# EVERYONE**CAN**COOK
## *seafood*

ERIC AKIS

# EVERYONE**CAN**COOK
## *seafood*

whitecap

Edited by Elaine Jones
Proofread by Lesley Cameron
Cover and interior design by Jacqui Thomas
Photography by Michael Tourigny
Food styling by Eric Akis assisted by Laura Agnew

Printed and bound in Canada

**Library and Archives Canada Cataloguing in Publication**

Akis, Eric, 1961-
        Everyone can cook seafood / Eric Akis.
Includes index.

ISBN 1-55285-614-3

        1. Cookery (Seafood)  I. Title.
TX747.A43 2004              641.6'92              C2004-904591-1

The publisher acknowledges the financial support of the Government of Canada through the Book Publishing Industry Development Program for our publishing activities.

# EVERYONE CAN COOK
## *seafood*

CONTENTS

DEDICATION

To all those involved in harvesting the tasty riches of the sea in a safe and sustainable way. Without your efforts this book would be irrelevant. I also dedicate this book to the readers of my Victoria *Times Colonist* food columns and to the users of the recipes I create for Thrifty Foods. Your many positive comments over the years keep me energized and excited to create recipes that everyone can cook.


ACKNOWLEDGEMENTS

Once this book is on the shelf, I get all the glory. The truth is, though, a large group of dedicated and very creative people made my hopes and dreams for this book become a reality.

To absolutely everyone at Whitecap Books, from the proofreaders to the sales staff to the designers, thank you for making my work look so good, for being so professional and for being an absolute joy to work with.

To my friend and photographer, Michael Tourigny, and to his former assistant, Mandy Mainland, thank you for taking such great photos for the book and for helping me develop such a distinct look for them.

To Elaine Jones, thank you for brilliantly editing this book and for all your fine suggestions on improving its content.

Thank you to Carolyn Heiman, Features Editor at the Victoria *Times Colonist*, for continuing to hone my writing skills. Your efforts have made writing concise cookbooks a whole lot easier.

To Ralf Mundel, Alex Campbell Jr. and everyone else at Thrifty Foods, thank you for being so unbelievably supportive of my attempts to make *Everyone Can Cook Seafood* a smashing success.

Thanks to the ultra-efficient Alison Field, who also assisted me with my first book, for helping out with those darn metric conversions and with the initial layout of the recipes.

Finally, thanks to my darling wife, Cheryl, and my "gosh can he eat" teenage son, Tyler, for loving and believing in me. I'm a lucky man.

# Introduction

No matter where I travel, whether it's Toronto, San Francisco, St. John's, Houston or Vancouver, restaurants that serve great seafood are always packed.

People love seafood. The irony is that when many of those diners get home, they'll go back to eating meat and potatoes. Time and time again, people tell me they'd eat more seafood, but they don't know how to cook it. They don't know what to buy; if it's fresh they don't know how to store it; if it's live, they're squeamish about it. Many are afraid they'll overcook it or don't know how to flavour it.

*Everyone Can Cook Seafood* demystifies seafood cookery. It answers these concerns and many more with informative sidebars, step-by-step instructions and easy-to-follow recipes. This book is designed to make the home cook feel confident about cooking seafood, whether it's for a special occasion or Tuesday supper.

I decided to write this book after reviewing several other seafood cookbooks. None were dedicated to all levels of cooks, particularly those with little or no knowledge. My first book, *Everyone Can Cook*, targeted this group with a broad selection of "I can do this" kind of recipes. There must have been a need; the book became a best-seller a few months after its release.

*Everyone Can Cook Seafood* carries forward the principles that made the first book popular, offering recipes that work using easily accessible ingredients. The recipes offer flexibility too. Each one has options for tweaking the dish to widen its use, heighten the flavour or simply make it more to your liking. Many recipes meet the need for dishes that can be created quickly, but still have flavour and flair. Others challenge, but don't intimidate—perfect for those who do not mind spending a little extra time on a dish if they know the end results will be worth it.

The mouth-watering photographs of the recipes in this book show dishes a home cook can prepare—not over-the-top presentations that only a professional chef could put on the table. They'll make you want to put on your apron and start cooking!

Today's supermarkets and fish markets offer an array of seafood never seen before. With *Everyone Can Cook Seafood* at hand, home cooks will have the inspiration and the instructions to serve up their catch.

# SEAFOOD TO START

# Crunchy Sesame Shrimp with Ginger Plum Sauce

preparation time · 30 minutes
cooking time · 10 minutes
makes · 18 pieces

Sweet, slightly nutty sesame seeds give the shrimp a heavenly crunch. Two to three of these shrimp make a perfect appetizer-sized portion.

**NOTE**
The plum sauce used in this recipe is the Chinese-style variety sold in the Asian foods aisle at most supermarkets.

| | | |
|---|---|---|
| 1 cup | plum sauce | 250 mL |
| 1 Tbsp. | chopped fresh ginger | 15 mL |
| 2 Tbsp. | soy sauce | 25 mL |
| 1/3 cup | cornstarch | 75 mL |
| 2 | large eggs beaten with 2 Tbsp. (25 mL) water | 2 |
| 1 cup | sesame seeds | 250 mL |
| 18 | large shrimp, peeled, leaving tail portion intact, and deveined | 18 |
| to taste | salt and white pepper | to taste |
| | vegetable oil | |

Place the plum sauce, ginger and soy sauce in a small pot. Slowly heat through over low heat. Meanwhile, place the cornstarch, egg mixture and sesame seeds in three separate shallow plates or bowls. Season the shrimp with salt and white pepper. Coat in cornstarch, shaking off the excess. Dip the shrimp in the beaten egg mixture and coat it evenly. Roll it in the sesame seeds, gently pressing the seeds on.

Heat 1/4 inch (5 mm) of oil in a large skillet over medium-high heat. Cook the shrimp, in batches if necessary, for 2 minutes per side, or until golden and cooked through. (Reduce the temperature if the shrimp brown too quickly.) Drain on paper towels, then arrange the shrimp on appetizer plates or on a platter, with a bowl of the warm sauce alongside for dipping.

## BUYING AND HANDLING SHRIMP AND PRAWNS

In seafood markets on the west coast of Canada and the northwestern United States, the term prawn is used to describe large shrimp. However, in the rest of North America the term shrimp is used to describe the species, no matter what the size. To keep things consistent, and also because I was born in eastern Canada and grew up with the term, in this book I've used the term shrimp throughout.

Shrimp are priced and categorized according to size. This is determined by what is called the "count"—the number they yield per pound, once the head is removed. Jumbo are 11–15 per pound, extra-large 16–20, large 21–30, medium 31–35 and small 36–45.

Unless they come from nearby waters, the raw shrimp found in the fresh seafood case at supermarkets are previously frozen. Although there are variations in texture and flavour, the different sizes can be substituted for one another.

Raw and fresh-cooked shrimp are highly perishable. Use them within one day of purchase. Once home, remove them from the packaging and place in a bowl; cover them and store in the coldest part of the fridge until needed. Never store them in the plastic bag or plastic-wrapped container they are sold in, as shrimp tend to sweat, which negatively affects flavour.

**ERIC'S OPTIONS**
Other seafood, such as large scallops or small, boneless fish fillets, can also be coated this way. For spicy plum sauce, add Asian-style chili sauce to taste.

# Mini Shrimp Cocktail

preparation time · 10 minutes
cooking time · none
makes · 12 servings

I serve these miniature versions of the classic appetizer at our annual Christmas open house. They are quick to make and always eagerly devoured by guests.

**ERIC'S OPTIONS**
To make crab cocktail, replace the shrimp with an equal amount of cooked, well-drained crabmeat. To make an assorted seafood cocktail, use a mix of cooked seafood.

| | | |
|---|---|---|
| 1 1/2 cups | baby salad greens or shredded head lettuce | 375 mL |
| 10 oz. | cooked salad shrimp, well chilled | 300 g |
| | cocktail sauce, store-bought or homemade (see page 169) | |
| | small lemon slices and parsley sprigs for garnish | |

Divide the salad greens or shredded lettuce among 12 small, decorative glasses. (A port or sherry glass works well.) Place the shrimp on top of the lettuce. (The cocktail can be made to this stage several hours in advance; wrap and store in the fridge until needed.) Top the shrimp with a small spoonful of cocktail sauce. Garnish with a lemon slice and parsley sprig and serve.

### DEVEINING AND PEELING SHRIMP

Whether or not to remove the dark intestinal vein that runs down the centre of shrimp, a technique called deveining, depends on their size. In general, small and medium-sized shrimp do not need deveining except for aesthetic purposes. However, the veins of larger shrimp often contain grit and should be removed.

If cooking larger shrimp with the shell on, make a lengthwise slit along the back of the shell with kitchen scissors to expose the flesh. With a paring knife, make a shallow slit down the centre of the flesh. Pull out the dark vein, or rinse it out with cold water. To peel and then devein, hold the tail of the shrimp in one hand, slip the thumb of your other hand under the shell between its swimmerets (its little legs), and then pull off the shell, leaving the very bottom portion of the tail intact. Remove the vein as described above.

# Shrimp
# Bloody Marys

preparation time · 10 minutes
cooking time · 2–3 minutes
makes · 4 servings

Here's a tasty cocktail and an appetizer all in one glass.

ERIC'S OPTIONS
Make a shrimp
Caesar by replacing
the tomato juice
with clamato juice.

| | | |
|---|---|---|
| 8 | large shrimp | 8 |
| 6 oz. | vodka | 175 mL |
| dash | Worcestershire and hot pepper sauce | dash |
| grind | freshly cracked black pepper | grind |
| 24 oz. | tomato juice | 750 mL |
| 4 | small celery stalks | 4 |
| 4 | lemon wedges | 4 |

Cook the shrimp in a pot of lightly salted boiling water until just cooked, about 2–3 minutes. Drain, place in ice-cold water to chill, and then drain well. Peel the shrimp, leaving the tip of the tail attached. Devein, if desired (see page 12).

Fill 4 tall glasses half-full with ice cubes. Divide the vodka among the glasses, and then add the Worcestershire, hot pepper sauce and black pepper. Pour in the tomato juice. Garnish each drink with a celery stalk and lemon wedge. Hook two shrimp on the rim of each glass and serve.

# Prosciutto-Wrapped Scallops with Pesto Mayonnaise

preparation time · 20 minutes
cooking time · 8–10 minutes
makes · 4 servings

Wrapping scallops in prosciutto offers a more intriguing, Italian-style taste, and is a less fatty alternative to streaky bacon.

**ERIC'S OPTIONS:**
You can substitute large shrimp or medium shucked oysters for a delicious alternative to scallops. Cooking time remains the same.

| | | |
|---|---|---|
| 1/2 cup | mayonnaise | 125 mL |
| 2 Tbsp. | pesto (homemade or store-bought) | 25 mL |
| to taste | salt, white pepper and lemon juice | to taste |
| 12 | large sea scallops | 12 |
| 6 | paper-thin slices prosciutto, each cut in half lengthwise | 6 |

Combine the mayonnaise, pesto, salt, pepper and lemon juice in a small bowl. Cover and set aside in the fridge. Preheat the oven to 425°F (220°C).

Wrap a half piece of prosciutto around the outer edge of each scallop. Secure with a toothpick, if necessary. Place on a non-stick or parchment-lined baking sheet. Bake for 8–10 minutes, or until just cooked through. Arrange on appetizer plates or a platter, with a bowl of the mayonnaise alongside for dipping.

# Hot Crab and
# Asparagus Canapés

| preparation time | · | 30 minutes |
| cooking time | · | 10 minutes |
| makes | · | 16–20 pieces |

You can use canned, frozen or fresh crabmeat to make these elegant, hot and appetizing canapés.

**NOTE**
To blanch the asparagus, cook it in boiling water for 1–2 minutes. Drain, chill in ice water, then drain again.

| | | | |
|---|---|---|---|
| 1 | 1/2-lb. (250g) package hard cream cheese at room temperature | 1 |
| 1 cup | crabmeat, drained and squeezed of excess moisture | 250 mL |
| 1 | garlic clove, finely chopped | 1 |
| 2 | green onions, finely chopped | 2 |
| to taste | salt, lemon juice and hot pepper sauce | to taste |
| 16–20 | 1/4-inch (5-mm) thick baguette slices | 16–20 |
| 16–20 | small asparagus spears, blanched and cut in half lengthwise | 16–20 |
| 1/4 cup | freshly grated Parmesan cheese | 50 mL |

Preheat the oven to 400°F (200°C.) Beat the cream cheese until light. Beat in the crab, garlic and green onions until just combined; season with salt, lemon juice and hot pepper sauce. Spread the mixture on the baguette slices and then place the slices on a non-stick or parchment-lined baking tray. Top each canapé with two half asparagus spears, cut-side down, overlapping them slightly. Sprinkle with a little Parmesan cheese. Bake for 10 minutes or until heated through. Arrange on a platter and serve.

### ERIC'S OPTIONS
These canapés can be made several hours in advance and stored, loosely wrapped, in the fridge. Because you'll be baking from cold, allow 3–4 minutes extra cooking time. Make hot shrimp and asparagus canapés by replacing the crab with an equal amount of cooked salad shrimp, finely chopped. For a hot dip to use with vegetables or bread cubes, double the crabmeat mixture, blend in 1/2 cup (125 mL) of mayonnaise and omit the asparagus. Place in a heatproof bowl and cover and bake or microwave until heated through.

# Raw Oysters with Chive Horseradish Vinaigrette

preparation time · 20 minutes (depending how fast you can shuck)
cooking time · none
makes · 4 servings

This fresh, lively tasting vinaigrette wonderfully compliments the salty, sometimes cucumber-like, taste of raw oysters.

**ERIC'S OPTIONS**
If you like things spicy, use extra-hot horseradish in the vinaigrette. If chives are unavailable, use finely chopped green onions instead. For an interesting herbal licorice taste, replace the chives with chopped fresh tarragon.

| | | |
|---|---|---|
| 12 | small oysters, shucked and left in the half shell (see How to Buy and Shuck an Oyster, page 17) | 12 |
| 2 Tbsp. | olive oil | 25 mL |
| 1 Tbsp. | snipped fresh chives | 15 mL |
| 2 tsp. | horseradish, or to taste | 10 mL |
| 2 Tbsp. | finely chopped red bell pepper | 25 mL |
| pinch | sugar | pinch |
| to taste | salt and lemon juice | to taste |

Place the oysters on small appetizer plates or arrange on a platter. Place the remaining ingredients in a bowl and mix well to combine. Spoon a little vinaigrette over each oyster. Serve immediately.

Crunchy Sesame Shrimp
with Ginger Plum Sauce   page 10

Mini Shrimp
Cocktail   page 12

Shrimp Bloody
Marys  page 13

Prosciutto-Wrapped Scallops
with Pesto Mayonnaise   page 14

Baked Oysters with
Spinach and Parmesan   page 18

Smoked Tuna on
Green Onion Pancakes   page 23

Deep-Fried Calamari with
Basil Garlic Dipping Sauce   page 24

Bouillabaise page 30

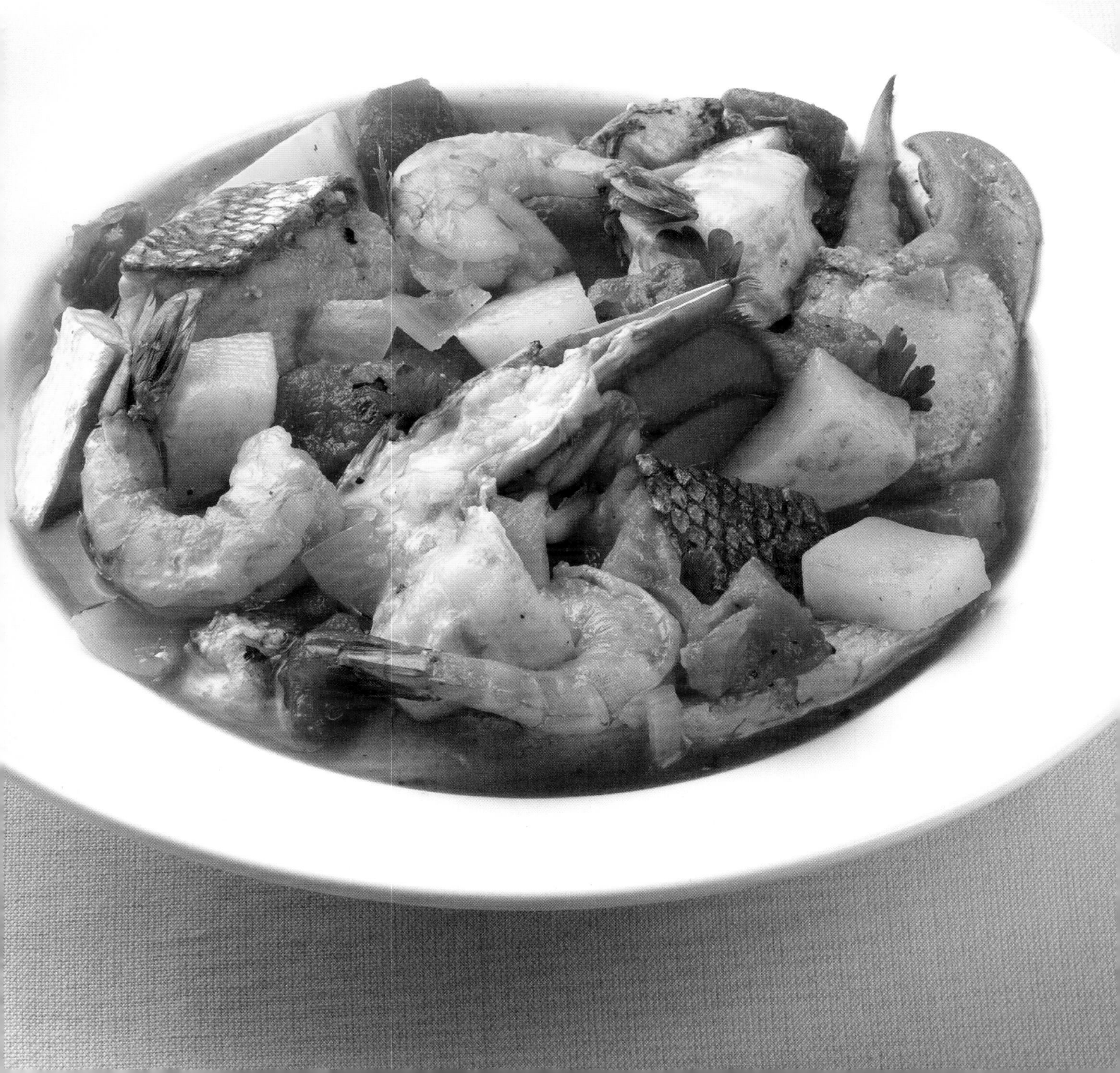

### HOW TO BUY AND SHUCK AN OYSTER

When buying oysters, choose those with tightly closed shells that are heavy for their size—an indication they still contain their precious juice. Small oysters are ideal for eating raw, while medium to large ones are best for cooking. It's best to use oysters soon after purchase, but if you do have to store them for a day, place them in a shallow container, cover them with a damp cloth and store in the coldest part of the fridge.

Scrub the oyster in cold water with a bristled brush. To shuck, place it on a slightly dampened kitchen towel, cupped side down with the hinged—more pointed—end facing you. Hold it in place with another kitchen towel. If desired, wear sturdy rubber gloves to protect your hands. Wedge the point of your oyster knife into the hinge of the shell. Work the knife in 1/4 inch (5 mm), and then twist it to pry the oyster open. Slide the knife across the top shell and remove and discard. Slide the knife under the oyster to detach it from the bottom shell. Remove any shell fragments and the oyster is ready to be used as desired.

# Baked Oysters with Spinach and Parmesan

preparation time · 20 minutes
cooking time · 10–12 minutes
makes · 4 servings

Rich-tasting oysters marry well with equally rich flavours. In this recipe spinach, cream and Parmesan cheese do the work deliciously.

**ERIC'S OPTIONS**
To help prevent the creamy spinach mixture from spilling out of the oyster shells during cooking, spread a thick layer of coarse sea salt on the baking sheet or roasting pan and nestle the shells into the salt until level.

| | | |
|---|---|---|
| 1/4 cup | dry white wine | 50 mL |
| 4 cups | stemmed spinach leaves, packed | 1 L |
| 1 | garlic clove, finely chopped | 1 |
| 1/2 cup | whipping cream | 125 mL |
| to taste | salt and white pepper | to taste |
| 12 | medium oysters, shucked and left in the half shell (see page 17) | 12 |
| 1/3–1/2 cup | freshly grated Parmesan cheese | 75–125 mL |

Preheat the oven to 450°F (230°C). Bring the wine to a boil in a large, wide skillet over medium-high heat. Add the spinach and cook until it just wilts and the wine and liquid from the spinach evaporate. Add the garlic and whipping cream and cook until the cream thickens slightly. Remove from the heat; season with salt and white pepper.

Place the oysters on a large baking sheet or roasting pan. Top each with a spoonful of the spinach mixture and sprinkle with Parmesan cheese. Bake for 10–12 minutes, until nicely browned and bubbling. Carefully lift the oysters onto 4 appetizer plates. Serve immediately.

# Vodka-Spiked Gravlax

| preparation time | · | 10 minutes plus marinating time |
| cooking time | · | none |
| makes | · | 6–8 servings |

Vodka, sugar and salt combine to flavourfully cure the salmon, "cooking" it without ever having to turn on the stove.

**ERIC'S OPTIONS**
For a slightly stronger, more distinct alcoholic taste, use gin, scotch or cognac instead of the more neutral-tasting vodka. For a more candied taste, use golden brown sugar, lightly packed, instead of granulated sugar.

| | | | |
|---|---|---|---|
| 2 | 1-lb. (500-g) centre-cut salmon fillets, skin on and pin bones removed | 2 | |
| 1 | small bunch dill (about 12–14 sprigs with stems attached) | 1 | |
| 2 oz. | vodka | 60 mL | |
| 3 Tbsp. | coarse sea or kosher salt | 45 mL | |
| 3 Tbsp. | sugar | 45 mL | |
| 1 Tbsp. | coarsely cracked white or black peppercorns | 15 mL | |

Place one piece of the salmon skin-side down in a glass dish. Arrange the dill evenly over top. Drizzle with the vodka. Mix the salt, sugar and peppercorns in a bowl; sprinkle evenly over the dill. Top with the other piece of salmon, placing it skin-side up and fitting it on top so the two stacked pieces of fish lie flat. Cover with plastic wrap and then foil. Set a small board on top of the salmon and weight it with something weighing about 5 lbs. (2.2 kg). Cans of food work well. Marinate in the fridge for 48–72 hours. (The longer the salmon is cured the more "cooked" it becomes.) Turn the adjoined salmon pieces over and baste with the accumulated juices every 12 hours.

To serve, remove the fish from the marinade, scrape away the flavourings and pat the fish dry. Cut into thin slices at a 45-degree angle. Gravlax makes a delicious appetizer or sandwich when served on rye bread and topped with thinly sliced onions, capers, dill and horseradish or sour cream.

# Smoked Salmon Pâté

| preparation time | · | 5 minutes |
| cooking time | · | none |
| makes | · | 1 3/4 cups (425 mL), serves 6–8 as an appetizer |

This delicious pâté can be quickly whipped up in the food processor. To make a simple, but elegant canapé, pipe the pate on small rounds of rye bread and garnish with sprigs of dill and tiny lemon wedges.

**ERIC'S OPTIONS**
For a lower-fat pâté use light versions of the cream cheese and sour cream. The pâté won't be as thick, but it will still be very tasty.

| | | |
|---|---|---|
| 1 | 1/2-lb. (250-g) package hard cream cheese, at room temperature | 1 |
| 4 oz. | cold- or hot-smoked salmon, bones and skin removed, coarsely chopped | 125 g |
| 2 Tbsp. | sour cream | 25 mL |
| 2 tsp. | chopped fresh dill | 10 mL |
| 1 Tbsp. | horseradish, or to taste | 15 mL |
| 1 Tbsp. | lemon juice | 15 mL |
| to taste | salt and white pepper | to taste |

Place the cream cheese, smoked salmon, sour cream, dill, horseradish and lemon juice in a food processor; pulse until a coarse pâté forms. Season with salt and pepper; pulse until smooth. Spoon into a serving bowl and serve with sliced bread and crackers.

## COLD- AND HOT-SMOKED SALMON

There are two main types of smoked salmon: cold-smoked and hot-smoked.

Cold-smoked salmon is smoked at temperatures ranging from 70° to 90°F (21°–32°C). Before smoking, the salmon is cured in salt brine, which has preservative and antiseptic properties. Cold-smoking gives the salmon a pleasant, smoky flavour and a silky, luscious texture. This style of smoked salmon is most often used in cold preparations—on bagels, tea sandwiches, canapés, sushi or served on its own with a few simple accompaniments.

Hot-smoked salmon is smoked and cooked at temperatures ranging from 120°–180°F (49°–82°C), depending on the desired flavour intensity and the size of the fish. Salt and other flavourings, such as sugar, spices and herbs, often in the form of brine, are used to boost flavour. Hot-smoked salmon is much firmer in texture than cold-smoked and can be enjoyed on its own as a snack or appetizer. It can be also be used in a range of cooked and uncooked dishes, such as pasta, soup, quiche, sandwich fillings, salads and pâté.

# Snow Peas
# in Smoked Salmon

preparation time · 20 minutes
cooking time · 30 seconds
makes · 12 pieces

Silky cold-smoked salmon and crunchy snow peas make a luscious textural contrast in this colourful and easy-to-make Asian-style appetizer.

**NOTE**

To blanch the snow peas, plunge them in boiling water until just tender, about 30 seconds. Drain well, cool in ice water, drain well again and pat dry.

**ERIC'S OPTIONS**

To give the teriyaki sauce an added bite, mix in wasabi paste or powder to taste. This appetizer can be made several hours in advance and stored in the fridge until you're ready to serve.

| | | |
|---|---|---|
| 12 | thin slices cold-smoked salmon | 12 |
| 12 | large snow peas, blanched | 12 |
| 1 cup | daikon or sunflower sprouts | 250 mL |
| 1/3 cup | teriyaki sauce | 75 mL |

Place a slice of salmon flat on a work surface. Place a snow pea and a small bunch of the sprouts near the end of the slice. Roll the smoked salmon around the filling, and set on a serving tray. Repeat with the remaining salmon, snow peas and sprouts. Pour the teriyaki sauce into a small bowl and use as a dip.

# Smoked Tuna
## on Green Onion Pancakes

| | | |
|---|---|---|
| preparation time | · | 30 minutes |
| cooking time | · | 4–5 minutes |
| makes | · | 24 pieces |

Serve this upscale finger food with a well-chilled glass of sparking wine or dry vodka martini. Velvety cold-smoked tuna is available at many retail outlets selling high-quality seafood.

| | | |
|---|---|---|
| 3/4 cup | all-purpose flour | 175 mL |
| 2 tsp. | baking powder | 10 mL |
| 3/4 cup | milk | 175 mL |
| 1 | large egg, beaten | 1 |
| 1/4 cup | finely chopped green onion | 50 mL |
| 1 tsp. | grated lemon zest | 5 mL |
| to taste | salt | to taste |
| 2 Tbsp. | vegetable oil | 25 mL |
| 1/3 cup | sour cream | 75 mL |
| 2 tsp. | Dijon mustard | 10 mL |
| 12 | thin slices cold-smoked tuna, each cut in half lengthwise | 12 |
| to taste | freshly cracked black pepper | to taste |
| | thin slices green onion for garnish | |

Combine the flour and baking powder in a bowl. Combine the milk, egg, green onion, lemon zest and salt in another. Add the dry mixture to the wet and mix until just combined. Heat the oil over medium to medium-high in a non-stick, electric griddle or a large non-stick skillet. Pour in the batter, making portions about 2 inches (5 cm) in diameter. Flip the pancakes once they begin to bubble on top. Cook for 1–2 minutes on the other side. Cool the pancakes to room temperature, then arrange on a serving tray. Combine the sour cream and mustard in a small bowl. Place small spoonfuls of the mixture in the centre of each pancake. Top each pancake with a half-slice of the smoked tuna. Sprinkle with pepper, garnish with a slice of green onion and serve.

# Deep-Fried Calamari
# with Basil Garlic Dipping Sauce

preparation time · 10–30 minutes (depending on type of calamari purchased)
cooking time · 2–3 minutes
makes · 4 servings

Tangy buttermilk's thick, almost sticky, consistency helps the flour adhere to squid rings. This encases the squid, also called calamari, in a batter-like way, helping to create an invitingly crispy exterior when deep-fried.

**NOTE**
Sliced, ready-to-use squid rings are sold frozen in many supermarkets and seafood stores. Thaw and pat dry before using.

| | | |
|---|---|---|
| 1/2 cup | mayonnaise | 125 mL |
| 3 Tbsp. | chopped fresh basil | 45 mL |
| 2 | garlic cloves, crushed | 2 |
| to taste | hot pepper sauce, salt and white pepper | to taste |
| | vegetable oil for deep-frying | |
| 1 cup | buttermilk | 250 mL |
| 1 1/2 cups | all-purpose flour seasoned with salt and pepper | 375 mL |
| 1 1/2 lbs. | sliced squid rings | 750 g |
| 1 | small red onion, finely chopped | 1 |
| | fresh basil leaves and lemon wedges for garnish | |

To make the dipping sauce, place the mayonnaise, basil, garlic, hot pepper sauce, salt and white pepper in a small bowl and mix to combine. Cover and store in the fridge until needed.

Preheat the oven to 200°F (95°C). Fill your deep-fryer with oil and heat to 375°F (190°C). Place the buttermilk and seasoned flour in separate bowls. Working in batches, dip the squid rings into the buttermilk, coating them well. Dredge the squid in the flour, shaking off the excess. Deep-fry the squid until lightly golden and crisp, about 2–3 minutes, then drain on paper towels. Keep warm in the oven until all are cooked. Pile the squid on serving plates or in shallow bowls. Sprinkle with the chopped onion and garnish with basil and lemon wedges. Serve the dipping sauce alongside.

## FACTS ABOUT SQUID

Squid, also called calamari, has gone from being a menu item once limited to a few ethnic restaurants to one offered by countless mainstream establishments, including my local pub.

Beyond its appealing taste, squid is also inexpensive, nutritious and low in fat. When you put all these positives together you begin to wonder why more people don't cook it at home. I know the answer: they don't know how. This is not surprising because squid, with its elongated body tipped with tentacles, seems exotic and gives the impression it must be hard to prepare.

The cleaning part of the equation is what turns some away from cooking squid. But cleaning whole squid is not all that difficult—although it is a bit time consuming.

Start by pulling the head and tentacles away from the body. Cut the tentacles away from the head, just above the hard, ball-shaped beak found inside it. Discard the head. Reach inside the squid body and pull out the plastic-like quill and discard. Using your fingers, peel off the skin. This can also be done under cold water, which sometimes makes it easier to remove. Scrape the skin off with a small knife if it's particularly tough to get off. The squid tentacles and tube are now ready to be used.

If you are squeamish about cleaning squid, don't worry—seafood producers solved that problem years ago by selling squid that's cleaned and ready to use. And if you're not good with a knife you can even buy it already sliced into rings or cut Asian-style (the flesh is scored and takes on a diamond pattern once cooked).

The length of time you should cook squid has been summed up by some cooking professionals like this: "Cook it for two minutes or two hours. At high temperatures, such as stir-frying, deep-frying or steaming, squid will cook in 2 to 3 minutes or less. You just want it to lose its rawness. If you go beyond that it will become tough and chewy and turn into what some call 'nature's chewing gum'."

In braised or stewed dishes, long, slow cooking is required. As it simmers slowly in the flavouring liquid it tenderizes just like tough stewing meat would in a similar situation.

Thaw frozen squid in the fridge overnight or in cold water before using it. Purchase fresh squid the same day you intend to use it.

**ERIC'S OPTIONS**
Instead of using store-bought, pre-sliced squid rings, use 1 1/2 lbs. (750 g) squid tubes, sliced into 1/2-inch (1-cm) rings. Or use 3 lbs. (1.5 kg) whole squid, cleaned, bodies cut into 1/2-inch (1-cm) rings, and tentacles left intact. If fresh basil is not available, use other fresh herbs, such as chives, parsley, dill or oregano, adjusting the amount according to your taste.

# Chilled Mussels
# with Lemon Tarragon Drizzle

preparation time · 20 minutes
cooking time · 3–4 minutes
makes · 4 servings

These tangy, mussels make an easy, inexpensive appetizer on a hot summer night.

| THE DRIZZLE | | | |
|---|---|---|---|
| | 2 Tbsp. | lemon juice | 25 mL |
| | 2 tsp. | Dijon mustard | 10 mL |
| | 1 | garlic clove, crushed | 1 |
| | 2 tsp. | finely chopped fresh tarragon | 10 mL |
| | pinch | sugar | pinch |
| | 1/4 cup | extra virgin olive oil | 50 mL |
| | to taste | salt and freshly cracked black pepper | to taste |
| THE MUSSELS | | | |
| | 1/2 cup | dry white wine | 125 mL |
| | 1 | garlic clove, chopped | 1 |
| | 24 | large mussels, washed well, beards removed | 24 |
| | 6–8 | butter or leaf lettuce leaves | 6–8 |
| | for garnish | fresh tarragon sprigs | for garnish |

### THE DRIZZLE

Place all the ingredients in a bowl and whisk well to combine. Cover and set aside until the mussels are ready.

### THE MUSSELS

Place the wine and garlic in a pot and bring to a boil. Add the mussels, cover and cook until they just open. Drain the mussels well, spread on a large tray and cool to room temperature. Arrange the lettuce on a large platter. Remove the top shell from each mussel and discard. Arrange the meat-filled halves of the mussels on the platter. Chill in the fridge for at least 1 hour. Drizzle with the lemon/tarragon mixture, garnish with the tarragon sprigs, and serve.

### HOW TO CLEAN A MUSSEL

Just before cooking, clean wild mussels by scrubbing under cold water with a stiff brush. Cultivated mussels are washed thoroughly before being shipped to wholesalers and retailers, so they only need to be rinsed in cold water before cooking. Pull off the "beard," the hair-like filaments the mussel uses to attach itself to rocks and other surfaces, and the mussels are ready for cooking.

### ERIC'S OPTIONS

Substitute other herbs, such as dill or chives, for the tarragon in the drizzle. For a sweeter taste, use orange juice instead of lemon.

# STIRRING SOUPS

CHAPTER TWO

# Bouillabaisse

| preparation time | · | 40 minutes |
| cooking time | · | about 40 minutes |
| makes | · | 4–6 servings |

This hearty Mediterranean-style soup makes a fine and filling meal. To maximize flavour and texture, use several kinds of fish when making it, such as cod, halibut, sole and salmon.

**ERIC'S OPTIONS**

For a less expensive alternative, replace the lobster with 18–24 mussels or clams, or a mix of both. Add them when you add the shrimp, and cook just until they open. Rouille, a rich, spicy sauce, is traditionally spooned into bowls of bouillabaisse to boost the flavour even more. I make a quick version of it in the food processor by blending together 3/4 cup (175 mL) mayonnaise, a roasted red pepper, 2 chopped garlic cloves and 1 slice of white bread, torn in pieces. Add salt, freshly cracked black pepper, cayenne pepper and lemon juice to taste.

| | | |
|---|---|---|
| 20–24 | medium shrimp | 20–24 |
| 2 1/2 cups | fish, chicken or vegetable stock | 625 mL |
| 3 Tbsp. | olive oil | 45 mL |
| 2 | garlic cloves, chopped | 2 |
| 2 | medium onions, chopped | 2 |
| 1 | 14-oz. (398-mL) can diced tomatoes | 1 |
| 2 Tbsp. | tomato paste | 25 mL |
| 1/2 tsp. | fennel seeds | 2 mL |
| 1/4–1/2 tsp. | crushed chili flakes | 1–2 mL |
| 1/2 tsp. | saffron threads | 2 mL |
| 3 | strips orange peel, about 1/2 x 3 inches (1 x 8 cm) | 3 |
| 1/2 tsp. | sugar | 2 mL |
| 3 | medium white-skinned potatoes, cut into 1/2-inch (1-cm) cubes | 3 |
| 1 1/2 lbs. | boneless fish fillets, cubed | 750 g |
| to taste | salt and freshly cracked black pepper | to taste |
| 1- to 1 1/2-lb. | live lobster, cleaned and cut into smaller pieces (see How to Cut Up a Live Lobster, page 31) | 500- to 750-g |
| 12–18 | baguette slices, brushed with olive oil and broiled until golden. | 12–18 |
| 2 Tbsp. | chopped parsley | 25 mL |

Rinse the shrimp in cold water and drain well. Peel, leaving the tip of the tail attached. Cover the shrimp and refrigerate. Place the shells in a pot with the stock. Add 3 cups (750 mL) of cold water. Bring to a boil, then reduce the heat to a gentle simmer. Cook for 20 minutes. Strain and discard the shells. Set the broth aside.

Heat the oil in a large, wide pot over medium heat. Add the garlic and onion and cook until tender, about 3–4 minutes. Add the broth, diced tomatoes, tomato paste, fennel seeds, chili flakes, saffron, orange peel, sugar and potatoes. Bring to a simmer and cook for 10 minutes. Add the cubed fish and cook for 3–4 minutes more. Add the peeled shrimp and the lobster pieces and cook 5 minutes longer, until the fish and shellfish are just cooked.

Divide the baguette slices among 4–6 large, shallow soup bowls. Spoon the bouillabaisse over top, ensuring that everyone gets a mix of seafood. Sprinkle with parsley and serve immediately.

HOW TO CUT UP A LIVE LOBSTER

Place the lobster on a plate and set it in the freezer, or submerge it in crushed ice, for 15 minutes. This more or less puts it to sleep, making it easier to cut. To do so, lay it belly-side down on a cutting board with the tail end opposite you. With one hand, grasp the tail where it joins the body. Hold the knife in the other hand and aim for a spot 1 inch (2.5 cm) from behind the eyes and equidistant from them. Insert the knife and cut through the head to the cutting board. This kills the lobster as quickly and painlessly as possible. Turn the lobster around and cut it in half through the tail. Rinse out the cavity. These half-lobster portions can be baked, steamed or grilled. To cut the lobster for dishes such as seafood stews, pasta dishes, stir-fries or Bouillabaisse, cut the tail and middle body portion into 3/4-inch to 1-inch (2- to 2.5-cm) pieces. Snap off each claw and crack it with the back side of a knife. Cut the lower portion of the claw in two.

# Hot and Sour Soup
## with Scallop Ribbons and Ginger

preparation time · 25 minutes
cooking time · about 10 minutes
makes · 4 servings

One spoon of this spicy, yet soothing, concoction will quickly lift your spirits inside and out. I like to serve it on cool, damp, dreary days.

**ERIC'S OPTIONS**
Egg is traditionally added to hot and sour soup. If you would like to add it to this version, do so after it has been thickened with the cornstarch. Beat 1 large egg in a bowl. Slowly pour the egg into the soup, gently stirring in a circular motion to create small ribbons of egg. When the egg is just cooked, it's time to serve the soup.

| | | |
|---|---|---|
| 4 cups | fish, chicken or vegetable stock | 1 L |
| 1/4 cup | rice vinegar | 50 mL |
| 3 Tbsp. | light soy sauce | 45 mL |
| 1 Tbsp. | Asian-style chili sauce, or to taste | 15 mL |
| 2 tsp. | sugar | 10 mL |
| 4 | medium fresh shiitake mushrooms, or 4 medium dried black Chinese mushrooms (soaked in warm water for 20 minutes to soften), stems removed and thinly sliced | 4 |
| 1 | small carrot, cut into thin, 1-inch long (2.5-cm) strips | 1 |
| 1-inch | piece peeled fresh ginger, sliced and cut into thin strips | 2.5-cm |
| 1 | garlic clove, chopped | 1 |
| 5 | large sea scallops, very thinly sliced | 5 |
| 1 | 10-oz. (280-g) package soft tofu, cut into small cubes or strips | 1 |
| 2 Tbsp. | cornstarch dissolved in 3 Tbsp. (45 mL) water | 30 mL |
| 2 | green onions, cut diagonally into thin strips | 2 |

Place the stock, vinegar, soy sauce, chili sauce and sugar in a pot and bring to a boil over high heat. Add the mushrooms, carrot, ginger and garlic, and adjust the heat to a gentle simmer. Cook for 5 minutes, or until the mushrooms and carrots are just tender. Add the scallops and tofu. Slowly stir in the cornstarch mixture. Simmer until the soup is lightly thickened and the scallops are just cooked through, about 2–3 minutes. Ladle the soup into bowls, sprinkle with the green onions and serve.

TYPES OF SCALLOPS

Although there are many species, scallops are usually classified into two main groups—bay scallops and sea scallops.

Bay scallops are quite small, usually about 1/2 inch (1 cm) in diameter. Their taste is sweet and succulent. Very tiny, about the size of a dime, calico scallops are sometimes sold as bay scallops, even though they are harvested from deep waters. They are mild tasting and less flavourful than bay and sea scallops.

Sea scallops, such as the world-famous Digby scallops harvested off the coast of Nova Scotia, are much larger than bay scallops. They average 1 1/2 inches (4 cm) in diameter. Their flavour is slightly sweet, rich and much more developed than bay scallops. Their colour ranges from off-white to creamy pink to pale beige.

Scallops are usually sold shucked, as they do not live long in the shell once out of the water. To maintain that "just harvested" taste, scallops are often quickly frozen.

Another type of scallop seen primarily on the west coast is the swimming scallop. These scallops use the motion caused by opening and closing their shells to flee from predators. The meat of swimming scallops is comparable in size to the bay scallop. The major difference is that swimming scallops are sold alive in the shell and cooked in the shell, similar to other bivalves, such as mussels and clams.

Scallops cook in just a few minutes, and should be tender to the bite when cooked. When overcooked they become tough and stringy.

# Lobster Bisque

| preparation time | · | 45 minutes |
|---|---|---|
| cooking time | · | about 45 minutes |
| makes | · | 4 servings |

I served this luscious soup to my wife when courting her with romantic dinners some 20 years ago. She said yes—what more do I need to say?

**ERIC'S OPTIONS**
To make crab bisque, replace the lobster with a whole, cooked Dungeness or snow crab weighing 1–1½ lbs. (500–750 g). Crack the shells and remove as much meat as you can. Rinse out the cavity. Cut or break the shells into smaller pieces and proceed as described for lobster bisque.

| | | |
|---|---|---|
| 1 | 1- to 1½-lb. (500- to 750-g) cooked lobster | 1 |
| 2 Tbsp. | olive oil | 25 mL |
| 2 | garlic cloves, sliced | 2 |
| 1 | small carrot, thinly sliced | 1 |
| 1 | celery rib, thinly sliced | 1 |
| 1 | small onion, thinly sliced | 1 |
| ½ cup | dry white wine | 125 mL |
| 4 cups | fish, chicken or vegetable stock | 1 L |
| 2 Tbsp. | tomato paste | 25 mL |
| 1 tsp. | dried tarragon | 5 mL |
| 1 | bay leaf | 1 |
| 3 Tbsp. | all-purpose flour | 45 mL |
| ½ cup | whipping cream | 125 mL |
| to taste | salt, white pepper and cayenne pepper | to taste |
| 2 oz. | brandy | 60 mL |
| 1 Tbsp. | chopped fresh parsley or chives | 15 mL |

Cut the lobster in half lengthwise. Rinse out the cavity, and then pull out the tail meat. Crack the legs and claws and remove the meat. Thinly slice the lobster meat and set aside in the fridge.

Cut or break the shells into smaller pieces. Heat the oil in a pot over medium heat. Add the shells, garlic, carrot, celery and onion and cook, stirring occasionally, for 5–6 minutes. Add the wine, $3^1/2$ cups (875 mL) of the stock, tomato paste, tarragon and bay leaf. Bring to a gentle simmer and cook 30–40 minutes. Strain the lobster stock into another pot. Bring back to a simmer. Mix the flour with the remaining $1/2$ cup (125 mL) of stock until it's smooth. Whisking steadily, slowly pour the mixture into the simmering stock. Gently simmer until the flour has cooked through and the soup has slightly thickened, about 5 minutes. Add the cream and reserved lobster. Season with salt, pepper and cayenne. Divide the brandy among 4 heated soup bowls. When the lobster is heated through, ladle the bisque into the bowls, sprinkle with parsley or chives and serve.

# Saffron-Scented
# Crab Consommé

preparation time · 40 minutes
cooking time · 30–35 minutes
makes · 4–6 servings

I serve this decadent, clear soup on special occasions, such as New Year's Eve. The unimpressive-looking egg white, crab shell and vegetable mixture clarifies the soup. It rises to the top and forms what chefs call a "cap," pulling the impurities out of the broth and making it clear.

**ERIC'S OPTIONS**
To make lobster consommé, replace the crab with a 1- to 1 1/2-lb. (500- to 750-g) cooked lobster. Proceed as described on the following page.

| | | |
|---|---|---|
| 1 | whole, cooked Dungeness or similar-sized crab, 1 1/4–1 1/2 lbs. (625–750 g) | 1 |
| 1/4 cup | finely diced carrot | 50 mL |
| 1/4 cup | finely diced onion | 50 mL |
| 1/4 cup | finely diced celery | 50 mL |
| 1 | garlic clove, thinly sliced | 1 |
| 3 | large egg whites | 3 |
| 1 | bay leaf | 1 |
| 5 cups | fish, chicken or vegetable stock | 1.25 L |
| 1/2 cup | dry white wine | 125 mL |
| 1/2 tsp. | saffron threads | 2 mL |
| to taste | salt and white pepper | to taste |
| 1 | green onion, cut into short, thin strips | 1 |
| 2 tsp. | chopped fresh tarragon or parsley | 10 mL |

Crack the crab shells and remove as much meat as you can. Reserve the crabmeat in the fridge. Rinse out the cavity. Cut or break the shells into smaller pieces and place in a bowl. Add the carrot, onion, celery, garlic, egg white and bay leaf. Mix to combine.

Place the stock, wine and saffron in a tall stockpot with a 6- to 8-inch (15- to 20-cm) diameter base. Stir in the egg white mixture. Set the pot over medium-high heat. Cook, stirring regularly, until the mixture just comes to a simmer. (Do not allow it to boil, or the soup will not become clear.) The moment it reaches a simmer, stop stirring and adjust the heat so the soup maintains a gentle simmer. Cook for 25–30 minutes, or until the liquid looks clear.

Line a fine mesh strainer with cheesecloth (sold in most supermarkets) and set it over another pot. Slightly tip the pot holding the consommé; the liquid will rise over the "cap" on the lower side. Use a small ladle to carefully scoop out the clear broth and strain into the other pot. (The soup can be made to this stage a day in advance. After cooling to room temperature, keep it and the reserved crabmeat in the fridge until needed.) Bring the consommé back to a simmer and season with salt and pepper. Divide the reserved crabmeat among 4–6 heated soup bowls. Sprinkle the green onions and tarragon or parsley over top. Ladle in the consommé and serve.

## FACTS ABOUT SAFFRON

Seafood and saffron are a match made in heaven. Try the Bouillabaisse (page 30), Saffron-Scented Crab Consommé (page 36) or Eric's Paella (page 76) and you'll soon understand what I mean. Saffron is the dried stigmas of a small purple crocus (*Crocus sativus*). Each flower provides only three stigmas and harvesting and drying them is very labour intensive. It takes approximately 14,000 stigmas to make 1 ounce (25 g) of saffron. No wonder it's the world's most expensive spice. But don't worry—a little goes a long way and you can buy it in small, reasonably priced packages good enough for three or four recipes. A pinch of saffron adds a wonderful aroma and a beautiful golden hue to any dish. The threads should be lightly crushed just before using. You can store saffron in an airtight container in a cool, dark place for up to 6 months.

# Sumptuous
# Seafood Chowder

preparation time · 25 minutes
cooking time · 20–25 minutes
makes · 4 servings

There is so much seafood in this chowder that it easily makes a meal when served with crackers or thick slices from a warm, crusty loaf.

**ERIC'S OPTIONS**
Substitute mussels for the clams, or use a combination. If you find this chowder too thick, simply thin with a little more stock, cream or milk.

| | | |
|---|---|---|
| 1/2 cup | dry white wine | 125 mL |
| 1 lb. | small fresh clams | 500 g |
| 3 Tbsp. | butter or vegetable oil | 45 mL |
| 1 | medium onion, finely chopped | 1 |
| 1 | celery rib, finely chopped | 1 |
| 2 | garlic cloves, chopped | 2 |
| 2 Tbsp. | all-purpose flour | 25 mL |
| 2 1/2 cups | fish, chicken or vegetable stock | 625 mL |
| 1/2 tsp. | dried thyme | 2 mL |
| 1 | bay leaf | 1 |
| 2 | medium red-skinned potatoes, cut into small cubes | 2 |
| 1/4 lb. | smoked salmon, chopped | 125 g |
| 1/4 lb. | small cooked shrimp | 125 g |
| 1/4 lb. | fresh, frozen (thawed) or canned crabmeat | 125 g |
| 1 cup | light cream or milk | 250 mL |
| to taste | salt and white pepper | to taste |
| 2 Tbsp. | chopped fresh parsley | 25 mL |

Bring the wine to a boil in a soup pot. Add the clams; cover and cook just until the clams open. Transfer the clams to a plate; strain and reserve the cooking liquid. When the clams are cool, remove the meat from the shells. Discard the shells and reserve the meat. Pour any liquid on the plate into the reserved cooking liquid.

Heat the butter or oil in the same pot over medium heat. Add the onion, celery and garlic and cook until tender, about 5 minutes. Sprinkle in the flour and mix well. Slowly stir in the reserved clam cooking liquid and the stock. Bring to a boil, then reduce the heat to a gentle simmer. Add the thyme, bay leaf, potatoes and smoked salmon and cook until the potatoes are just tender, about 10–15 minutes. Add the reserved clam meat, shrimp, crabmeat and cream or milk. Gently simmer for a few more minutes (do not boil). Season with salt and pepper, pour into bowls and sprinkle with chopped parsley just before serving.

# Tomato Soup
## with Mussels and Fresh Basil

| | | |
|---|---|---|
| preparation time | · | 25 minutes |
| cooking time | · | about 15 minutes |
| makes | · | 4 servings |

Tomato, garlic and basil give this eye-appealing soup Italian-style flare. It makes a greater starter, but you can also make a meal of it by serving it with warm slices of olive bread or focaccia.

ERIC'S OPTIONS
Make this soup with fresh clams instead of mussels. The procedure is the same; simply replace one mollusc for the other.

| | | |
|---|---|---|
| 24–30 | mussels | 24–30 |
| 1 Tbsp. | olive oil | 15 mL |
| 2 | garlic cloves, chopped | 2 |
| 1/2 cup | dry white wine | 125 mL |
| 1 | 28-oz. (796-mL) can crushed tomatoes | 1 |
| pinch | sugar | pinch |
| 2 cups | fish, chicken or vegetable stock | 500 mL |
| 2 Tbsp. | finely chopped fresh basil | 25 mL |
| 2 Tbsp. | finely chopped fresh parsley | 25 mL |
| 1/4 cup | freshly grated Parmesan cheese | 50 mL |
| to taste | salt and freshly cracked black pepper | to taste |

Wash the mussels in cold water and remove the beards (see How to Clean a Mussel, page 27). Heat the oil in a pot over medium-high heat. Add the garlic and cook for 1 minute.

Add the wine and bring to a boil. Add the mussels, cover and cook until they just open. Remove the mussels to a platter with a slotted spoon and set aside to cool to room temperature. Add the tomatoes, sugar and stock to the soup pot. Adjust the heat to a gentle simmer and cook for 10 minutes. Meanwhile, remove the top shell from each mussel and discard. Arrange the meat-filled halves in 4 soup bowls. When the soup has simmered 10 minutes, stir in half the basil, parsley and cheese; season with salt and pepper. Spoon the soup over the mussels. Sprinkle with the remaining basil, parsley and cheese, and serve.

# Thick and Creamy Clam Chowder

| | |
|---|---|
| preparation time | · 20 minutes |
| cooking time | · 20–25 minutes |
| makes | · 4 servings |

Canned clams are inexpensive and easy to use—two good reasons to make this hearty, "stick to your ribs" chowder.

**NOTE**
Clam nectar is often sold in cans. In some areas it is called clam juice.

**ERIC'S OPTIONS**
Regular milk, although not as rich or thick as condensed milk, can be used. For added colour, add 1/4 cup (50 mL) of finely diced carrot, and 1/4 cup (50 mL) of finely diced red bell pepper to the chowder with the onion and celery. If you prefer, use other herbs, such as dill or tarragon, instead of thyme.

| | | |
|---|---|---|
| 1 | 10-oz. (284-mL) can clams | 1 |
| 3 | strips bacon, finely chopped | 3 |
| 1 | small onion, finely chopped | 1 |
| 2 | celery ribs, finely chopped | 2 |
| 3 Tbsp. | all-purpose flour | 45 mL |
| 1 | 10-oz. (284-mL) can clam nectar | 1 |
| 1 | 13-oz. (385-mL) can 2% evaporated milk | 1 |
| 2 | medium potatoes, peeled and cubed | 2 |
| pinch | dried thyme | pinch |
| 1 | bay leaf | 1 |
| to taste | salt and white pepper | to taste |

Drain the clams, reserve the liquid and set both aside. Cook the bacon in a soup pot until slightly crispy. Add the onion and celery and cook, stirring, for 3–4 minutes. Mix in the flour until well combined. Slowly stir in the reserved clam juice, clam nectar and evaporated milk. Add the potatoes, thyme and bay leaf. Simmer for 10 minutes. Add the reserved clams, salt and pepper and simmer for 10 minutes more, or until the potatoes are tender.

# Smoked Haddock and New Potato Chowder

| | | |
|---|---|---|
| preparation time · | 20 minutes | |
| cooking time · | 25 minutes | |
| makes · | 4 servings | |

The fish, rather than the bacon used in some chowders, gives this "dinner in a bowl" an inviting, smoky taste.

**ERIC'S OPTIONS**
Substitute other smoked fish, such as salmon or cod, if smoked haddock is unavailable. If you don't care for a smoky taste, use fresh haddock instead of smoked. Although not as colourful, white-skinned new potatoes could be used in place of red.

| | | |
|---|---|---|
| 3 Tbsp. | butter | 45 mL |
| 1/2 | medium onion, finely chopped | 1/2 |
| 1/2 | medium green bell pepper, finely chopped | 1/2 |
| 1 | celery rib, finely chopped | 1 |
| 1 | garlic clove, chopped | 1 |
| 3 Tbsp. | all-purpose flour | 45 mL |
| 4 cups | milk | 1 L |
| 3 | medium red-skinned new potatoes, cubed | 3 |
| 1 | bay leaf | 1 |
| 1/2 lb. | smoked haddock fillets, bones and skin removed, cut into 1-inch (2.5-cm) cubes | 250 g |
| 2 tsp. | chopped fresh dill | 10 mL |
| to taste | salt and white pepper | to taste |

Melt the butter in a pot over medium heat. Add the onion, bell pepper, celery and garlic. Cook, stirring, for 3–4 minutes. Mix in the flour until well combined. Slowly stir in the milk and bring to a gentle simmer. Add the potatoes and bay leaf and cook, stirring occasionally, for 10 minutes. Add the smoked haddock and dill and simmer for 10 minutes more, or until the potatoes and fish are tender. Season with salt and pepper and serve.

# Salmon and Roasted Corn Soup

| | preparation time | · | 30 minutes |
|---|---|---|---|
| | cooking time | · | 45 minutes |
| | makes | · | 4–6 servings |

For optimum flavour, serve this soup in late summer when wild salmon and local corn are both in season.

| | | |
|---|---|---|
| 2 | cobs corn, kernels removed | 2 |
| 3 Tbsp. | olive oil | 45 mL |
| 1/2 | medium onion, diced | 1/2 |
| 1 | small red bell pepper, finely diced | 1 |
| 1/4 cup | all-purpose flour | 50 mL |
| 4 cups | fish, chicken or vegetable stock | 1 L |
| 1/2 lb. | boneless salmon fillet, skin removed and cubed | 250 g |
| 1 | bay leaf | 1 |
| 2 tsp. | fresh chopped thyme or 1/2 tsp. (2 mL) dried | 10 mL |
| 1/2 cup | whipping or light cream | 125 mL |
| 3 | green onions, finely chopped | 3 |
| to taste | salt and freshly cracked black pepper | to taste |

Preheat the oven to 400°F (200°C). Place the corn kernels in a single layer on a parchment-lined or non-stick baking tray. Roast for 20 minutes, or until the corn begins to caramelize and turn light brown around the edges. Remove from the oven and set aside.

Heat the oil in a soup pot over medium heat. Add the onion and bell pepper and cook for 3–4 minutes. Mix in the flour. Slowly pour in the stock, whisking steadily, until combined. Bring to a simmer, then stir in the salmon, bay leaf, thyme and roasted corn, reserving a little corn to garnish the top. Simmer for 20 minutes. Add the cream and green onions, reserving some of the latter to garnish the top. Bring the soup back to a simmer, but do not boil; season with salt and pepper. Ladle into bowls and garnish the top with the reserved corn and green onions.

# Chilled Crab and Avocado Soup

preparation time · 10 minutes
cooking time · none
makes · 4 servings

Crab and avocado are a match made in heaven. This rich and inviting soup makes an elegant lunch or starter on a hot summer day.

**ERIC'S OPTIONS**
Replace the crab with a similar amount of other shellfish, such as cooked salad shrimp, cooked langoustines (see What Are Langoustines?, page 53), or sliced lobster meat.

| | | |
|---|---|---|
| 2 | medium avocados, quartered, pitted and peeled | 2 |
| 2 1/2 cups | chicken or vegetable stock | 625 mL |
| 1/2 cup | light sour cream | 125 mL |
| 1 | lime, juice of, or to taste | 1 |
| 2 tsp. | curry powder, or to taste | 10 mL |
| to taste | salt | to taste |
| 1 cup | crabmeat | 250 mL |
| 2 Tbsp. | finely chopped yellow or red bell pepper | 25 mL |
| 2 Tbsp. | chopped cilantro or green onion | 25 mL |

Place the avocado, 1 cup (250 mL) of the stock and the sour cream in a food processor or blender. Pulse until smooth, then transfer to a bowl. Stir in the remaining stock and the lime juice, curry powder and salt. Chill the soup for at least 2 hours. Pour into chilled soup bowls. Divide the crabmeat among the bowls, setting it in the centre of the soup. Sprinkle with the bell pepper and cilantro or green onion and serve.

# Shrimp and Asparagus Soup

| preparation time | · | 20 minutes |
| cooking time | · | 25 minutes |
| makes | · | 4 servings |

I like to serve this soup to start off a spring dinner when fresh, local asparagus is at its finest.

**ERIC'S OPTIONS**
To make crab or lobster and asparagus soup, simply replace the shrimp with an equal amount of crabmeat or thinly sliced cooked lobster.

| | | |
|---|---|---|
| 3 Tbsp. | olive oil | 45 mL |
| 3/4 lb. | asparagus, trimmed and sliced | 375 g |
| 1/2 | medium onion, halved and sliced | 1/2 |
| 3 Tbsp. | all-purpose flour | 45 mL |
| 4 cups | fish, chicken or vegetable stock | 1 L |
| 1/3 lb. | cooked salad shrimp, plus some to decorate the top | 170 g |
| 1 Tbsp. | chopped fresh tarragon or dill | 15 mL |
| 1/2 cup | whipping or light cream | 125 mL |
| to taste | salt and white pepper | to taste |
| for garnish | tarragon or parsley sprigs | for garnish |

Heat the oil in a pot over medium heat. Add the asparagus and onion and cook, stirring, for 4–5 minutes. Mix in the flour until well combined. Slowly pour in the stock, whisking steadily, until all is combined. Bring to a simmer and cook until the asparagus is very tender, about 20 minutes.

Purée the mixture in a food processor or blender, and then return to the pot. Bring back to a gentle simmer, and then stir in the shrimp, tarragon or dill, and cream. Cook for 5 minutes more. Ladle the soup into bowls. Decorate the top of each serving with a few shrimp and a tarragon or parsley sprig.

# Fish
## Stock

preparation time · 20 minutes
cooking time · 30–35 minutes
makes · about 6 cups (1.5 L)

The bones of white fish, such as halibut, sole or flounder, are best for fish stock because they are not as oily as darker-fleshed species, like salmon or Arctic char. Stock from these fish will have a much stronger taste that can overpower a soup or sauce.

**ERIC'S OPTIONS**
If you do not want to use alcohol, simply omit the wine from the recipe. Add the herbs, water and bones all at the same time.

| | | |
|---|---|---|
| 2 Tbsp. | butter | 25 mL |
| 1 | large onion, halved and sliced | 1 |
| 1 | leek, halved lengthwise, washed well, and thinly sliced | 1 |
| 1 | celery rib, thinly sliced | 1 |
| 1 | medium carrot, thinly sliced | 1 |
| 1 cup | dry white wine | 250 mL |
| 1 | bay leaf | 1 |
| 6 | black peppercorns | 6 |
| 3–4 | fresh parsley sprigs | 3–4 |
| 8 cups | water | 2 L |
| 2 lbs. | white fish bones, washed and chopped | 1 kg |

Melt the butter in a soup pot over medium heat. Add the onion, leek, celery and carrot and cook until softened, but not coloured, about 4–5 minutes. Add the wine, bay leaf, peppercorns and parsley, and simmer until the wine has almost evaporated. Add the water and fish bones and bring to a simmer. Simmer for 20–25 minutes. The stock should have a mild, but attractive flavour when seasoned with salt and pepper. Simmer a little longer if it does not.

Strain through a sieve. The stock is now ready to use. Once cooled to room temperature it can be stored in the fridge for a few days or frozen for up to 2 months if stored in an air-tight container.

# SALADS&
# COLDDISHES

# Melon and Seafood
# Salad with Mint and Cumin

preparation time · 20 minutes
cooking time · none
makes · 4 appetizer-sized servings

A wine, martini or other decorative glass makes an elegant serving vessel for this light and colourful salad.

**ERIC'S OPTIONS**
If you don't have a melon baller, you can cut the fruit into 1/2-inch (1-cm) cubes instead. For a tropical taste, replace the melon balls with fresh pineapple, mango and papaya balls.

| | | |
|---|---|---|
| 2 | shallots, finely chopped | 2 |
| 1 Tbsp. | lemon juice | 15 mL |
| 1 Tbsp. | chopped fresh mint | 15 mL |
| 1/2 tsp. | ground cumin | 2 mL |
| to taste | salt and white pepper | to taste |
| 3 Tbsp. | olive oil | 45 mL |
| 4 oz. | cooked salad shrimp | 125 g |
| 4 oz. | fresh or tinned crabmeat, drained well | 125 g |
| 1 cup | honeydew melon balls | 250 mL |
| 1 cup | cantaloupe balls | 250 mL |
| 1 cup | seedless watermelon balls | 250 mL |
| 2–3 cups | baby salad greens | 500–750 mL |
| 4 | mint sprigs for garnish | 4 |

In a bowl, whisk together the shallots, lemon juice, mint, cumin, salt, pepper and olive oil. Add the shrimp, crabmeat and honeydew melon, cantaloupe and watermelon balls, and gently toss to combine. Marinate for 30 minutes in the fridge. Divide the greens among 4 decorative glasses. Spoon the salad on top. Garnish with mint sprigs and serve.

# Seashell Pasta Salad
# with Tuna and Bell Peppers

preparation time · 20 minutes
cooking time · 8–10 minutes
makes · 6–8 servings

This homestyle salad makes a nice side dish or colourful addition to a dinner buffet. It is also a nice lunch on its own when served on a bed of chopped lettuce.

**ERIC'S OPTIONS**
Make this salad with any other bite-sized pasta such as rotini, macaroni or bow-tie. For a more upscale salad, use a similar sized can of crabmeat instead of tuna. If you like, substitute other herbs, such as dill or parsley, for the tarragon.

| | | |
|---|---|---|
| 2 cups | small pasta shells | 500 mL |
| 1 | 6-oz. (170-g) can chunk tuna, drained and flaked | 1 |
| 1 | celery rib, finely chopped | 1 |
| 2 | green onions, finely chopped | 2 |
| 1/2 | medium red bell pepper, finely chopped | 1/2 |
| 1/2 | medium green bell pepper, finely chopped | 1/2 |
| 1/3 cup | mayonnaise | 75 mL |
| 2 Tbsp. | lemon juice | 25 mL |
| 2 tsp. | chopped fresh tarragon | 10 mL |
| 2 tsp. | horseradish | 10 mL |
| to taste | salt and white pepper | to taste |

Cook the pasta in a large of pot of lightly salted boiling water until just tender. Drain well, cool in cold water, drain well again, and place in a salad bowl. Add the remaining ingredients and mix gently to combine. Refrigerate the salad until ready to serve.

# Thai-Style Tuna Noodle Salad

preparation time · 30 minutes
cooking time · 1–2 minutes
makes · 4–6 servings

Rice noodles, peanuts and Asian-style chili sauce are just a few of the ingredients that give this salad a bright Thai-style taste.

**ERIC'S OPTIONS**
Replace the tuna with cooked seafood, such as salad shrimp or crabmeat or use Chinese-style egg noodles instead of rice noodles. The salad can be made several hours in advance and kept refrigerated until needed.

| | | |
|---|---|---|
| 1 Tbsp. | chopped fresh ginger | 15 mL |
| 2 | garlic cloves, crushed | 2 |
| 3 Tbsp. | light soy sauce | 45 mL |
| 1 Tbsp. | vegetable oil | 15 mL |
| 1 Tbsp. | sesame oil | 15 mL |
| 1 Tbsp. | rice vinegar | 15 mL |
| 1 Tbsp. | fresh lime juice | 15 mL |
| to taste | sugar | to taste |
| to taste | Asian-style chili sauce | to taste |
| 1 | 1/2-lb. (250-g) package rice noodles | 1 |
| 1 | 6-oz. (170-g) can chunk light tuna, drained well | 1 |
| 1 | small carrot, grated | 1 |
| 1 cup | grated cucumber or zucchini | 250 mL |
| 1 1/2 cups | bean sprouts | 375 mL |
| 2 | ripe, medium tomatoes, finely chopped | 2 |
| 3 | green onions, finely chopped | 3 |
| 1/3 cup | chopped cilantro | 75 mL |
| 1/2 cup | roasted peanuts, coarsely chopped | 125 mL |

Place the ginger, garlic, soy sauce, vegetable oil, sesame oil, rice vinegar, lime juice, sugar and chili sauce in a large bowl. Whisk to combine, then set aside.

Cook the rice noodles in boiling water until just tender, about 1–2 minutes. Drain well, cool in ice-cold water and drain well again. Add the noodles to the dressing. Add the tuna, carrot, cucumber or zucchini, bean sprouts, tomatoes and green onions. Gently toss to combine. Transfer the salad to a serving platter or to individual plates if serving as a main course. Sprinkle with cilantro and peanuts and serve.

# Langoustine and Citrus Salad

| preparation time | · | 20 minutes |
|---|---|---|
| cooking time | · | none |
| makes | · | 4 servings |

The flavours of citrus, cumin and mint give this refreshing, beautiful salad a Mediterranean-style taste.

**ERIC'S OPTIONS**
An equal amount of salad shrimp can be substituted for the langoustine. For added colour and a slightly sharper taste, replace one of the oranges with a peeled, halved and thinly sliced pink grapefruit. Overlap the grapefruit and orange slices when placing them on the plates.

| | | |
|---|---|---|
| 1 Tbsp. | lemon juice | 15 mL |
| 1 Tbsp. | lime juice | 15 mL |
| 1/2 tsp. | ground cumin | 2 mL |
| 1 Tbsp. | chopped fresh mint | 15 mL |
| to taste | salt and freshly cracked black pepper | to taste |
| pinch | cayenne pepper | pinch |
| 1/2 tsp. | sugar | 2 mL |
| 3 Tbsp. | olive oil | 45 mL |
| 3/4 lb. | cooked, peeled langoustine tails | 375 g |
| 2 | green onions, finely chopped | 2 |
| 1 | celery rib, finely chopped | 1 |
| 4 cups | baby salad greens | 1 L |
| 3 | medium oranges, peeled and thinly sliced | 3 |
| 4 | mint sprigs for garnish | 4 |

In a bowl, whisk together the lemon and lime juice, cumin, mint, salt, pepper, cayenne and sugar. Whisk in the oil. Add the langoustine tails, green onions and celery and mix gently to combine. Cover and marinate the mixture in the fridge for 30 minutes. Arrange the salad greens on 4 plates. Arrange the orange slices in a ring around the outer edge of the salad greens. Spoon the Langoustine mixture into the centre of the plate. Garnish with mint sprigs and serve.

WHAT ARE LANGOUSTINES?

Langoustine is the French word for prawn, and is also the name given to several varieties of deep-sea shellfish, also called scampi, that look like small lobsters or large shrimp and can be used in similar ways. Langoustines are sold whole, raw or cooked, either frozen or thawed from frozen. The tail portions are also available, sold raw, or cooked, shelled and ready to use. Look for langoustines in well-stocked supermarkets and specialty seafood stores.

# Salad Niçoise

| | | |
|---|---|---|
| preparation time | · | 20 minutes |
| cooking time | · | none |
| makes | · | 4 main dish servings; 6–8 side dish servings |

This classic southern French salad can be served as a main course when accompanied with a crusty baguette or loaf of olive bread—a fine meal to serve on the patio on a warm summer day.

**NOTE**
To blanch beans, plunge them in boiling water for 2 minutes. Drain well, cool in ice water, and drain well again.

| | | |
|---|---|---|
| 3 Tbsp. | red wine vinegar | 45 mL |
| 2 | garlic cloves, crushed | 2 |
| 2 tsp. | Dijon mustard | 10 mL |
| to taste | salt and freshly cracked black pepper | to taste |
| pinch | sugar | pinch |
| 1/2 cup | extra virgin olive oil | 125 mL |
| 2 | medium red- or white-skinned potatoes, cubed, cooked and cooled | 2 |
| 1/3 lb. | green beans, blanched and cooled | 170 g |
| 1/2 | English cucumber, halved lengthwise and sliced | 1/2 |
| 4 | medium, vine-ripened tomatoes, cut into small wedges | 4 |
| 1 | 6-oz. (170-g) can chunk tuna, drained well | 1 |
| 1/2 cup | niçoise or kalamata olives | 125 mL |
| 1 | head butter lettuce, separated into leaves | 1 |
| 4 | hard-boiled eggs, cut into quarters | 4 |
| 1 | bunch radishes, trimmed and thinly sliced | 1 |
| 2 Tbsp. | chopped fresh parsley | 25 mL |

Whisk the vinegar, garlic, mustard, salt, pepper and sugar in a large bowl. Slowly whisk in the olive oil. Add the potatoes, beans, cucumber, tomatoes, tuna and olives. Gently toss to combine. Cover and marinate the mixture for 30 minutes in the fridge. Line individual salad plates or a large serving platter or bowl with the lettuce leaves. Spoon the salad over top. Decorate the top with egg and radish slices; sprinkle with parsley. Serve immediately.

**ERIC'S OPTIONS**
For a special meal, use 3/4–1 lb. (375–500 g) of thick-cut fresh tuna steak instead of canned tuna. Brush with olive oil, season with salt and pepper and grill to medium rare, about 2–3 minutes per side. Cool to room temperature and slice or cube before adding to the salad.

# Spinach Salad with Lobster, Corn and Plum Tomatoes

| | | |
|---|---|---|
| preparation time | · | 15 minutes |
| cooking time | · | none |
| makes | · | 4 servings |

Cooked, whole lobsters are handy to use. You'll find them at well-stocked super-markets and seafood specialty stores.

**ERIC'S OPTIONS**
If you're not fond of spinach, make this salad with 6 cups (1.5 L) of baby salad greens or chopped romaine. Instead of lobster, you can use 20 cooked and peeled large shrimp.

| | | |
|---|---|---|
| 3 Tbsp. | extra virgin olive oil | 45 mL |
| 2 Tbsp. | white wine vinegar | 25 mL |
| 1 tsp. | Dijon mustard | 5 mL |
| 1 Tbsp. | chopped fresh tarragon | 15 mL |
| pinch | sugar | pinch |
| to taste | salt and freshly cracked black pepper | to taste |
| 1 | bunch fresh spinach, stemmed, washed and dried | 1 |
| 1 | 1- to 1 1/2-lb. (500- to 750-g) cooked lobster, meat removed from the shell and thinly sliced | 1 |
| 1 cup | corn kernels, fresh or frozen (thawed) | 250 mL |
| 3 | ripe plum tomatoes, cut into wedges | 3 |
| 1/4 cup | shaved Parmesan cheese | 50 mL |

Place the oil, vinegar, mustard, tarragon, sugar, salt and pepper in a salad bowl and whisk well to combine. Add the spinach and gently toss to coat with the dressing. Divide among 4 plates. Arrange the lobster, corn, tomatoes and Parmesan on top of the spinach. Serve immediately.

# Caesar Salad with Shrimp and Olive Bread Croutons

preparation time · 20 minutes
cooking time · 4–5 minutes
makes · 4–6 servings

Shrimp and olives add a tasty twist to this classic salad.

**ERIC'S OPTIONS**
Try making the croutons with other breads, such as focaccia or sourdough. For an iron-rich, more robust-tasting salad, replace the romaine with a large bunch of fresh spinach, stems trimmed, washed well and dried.

| | | |
|---|---|---|
| 2 Tbsp. | olive oil | 25 mL |
| 3 | 1/2-inch (1-cm) thick slices olive bread, cut into small cubes | 3 |
| 1/3 cup | mayonnaise | 75 mL |
| 2 | anchovies, finely chopped | 2 |
| 1 tsp. | Dijon mustard | 5 mL |
| 1–2 | garlic cloves, crushed | 1–2 |
| 1 tsp. | red wine vinegar | 5 mL |
| 2 tsp. | fresh lemon juice | 10 mL |
| to taste | Worcestershire sauce, hot pepper sauce and freshly ground black pepper | to taste |
| 1 | medium head romaine, washed, chopped and dried | 1 |
| 1/2 lb. | cooked salad shrimp | 250 g |
| 1/4 cup | freshly grated Parmesan cheese | 50 mL |
| 4 | lemon wedges | 4 |

Heat the oil in a large non-stick skillet over medium heat. Add the bread cubes and cook, stirring, until lightly toasted, about 5 minutes. Remove from the heat and set aside. Combine the mayonnaise, anchovies, Dijon mustard, garlic, vinegar, lemon juice, Worcestershire sauce, hot pepper sauce and pepper in a salad bowl. Add the romaine, shrimp and croutons and toss to combine. Divide the salad among individual plates, ensuring that some of the croutons and shrimp are on top. Sprinkle with the cheese, garnish with lemon and serve.

# Baked Chilled Salmon
# with Romaine, Olives and Oranges

preparation time · 30 minutes
cooking time · 12–15 minutes
makes · 2 servings

Salmon's fine flavour and firm texture is as enjoyable cold, as it is hot. In this main course salad it is deliciously paired with sweet oranges, crisp romaine lettuce and seductively salty olives.

| THE FISH | 2 | 5-oz. (150-g) salmon fillets | 2 |
|---|---|---|---|
| | 1 Tbsp. | extra virgin olive oil | 15 mL |
| | squeeze | lemon and orange juice | squeeze |
| | to taste | salt and white pepper | to taste |
| THE SALAD | 2 Tbsp. | extra virgin olive oil | 25 mL |
| | 2 Tbsp. | orange juice | 25 mL |
| | 2 tsp. | red wine vinegar | 10 mL |
| | to taste | salt and white pepper | to taste |
| | 3 cups | chopped romaine | 750 mL |
| | 1 | large orange, peel and pith removed, halved and sliced | 1 |
| | 12 | kalamata olives | 12 |
| | 1/2 | small red onion, thinly sliced | 1/2 |

### THE FISH

Preheat the oven to 400°F (200°C). Place the salmon in a non-stick or parchment-lined baking dish. Drizzle with the olive oil and lemon and orange juice; season with salt and pepper. Bake for 12–15 minutes, or until cooked through. Remove from the oven and cool to room temperature. Chill in the fridge for at least 2 hours.

### THE SALAD

In a salad bowl, whisk together the olive oil, orange juice, vinegar, salt and pepper. Add the romaine and gently toss to coat. Mound the romaine on 2 dinner plates. Decorate the top of the salad with orange slices, olives and red onion rings. Set the salmon in the centre and drizzle with any dressing left in the bowl.

**ERIC'S OPTIONS**
Substitute baby spinach or baby salad greens for the romaine. Top the salad with cooked, peeled and chilled large shrimp instead of salmon. You'll need 5 to 6 shrimp for each salad portion.

# Salmon Salad in Lettuce Cups

| preparation time | · | 20 minutes |
| cooking time | · | none |
| makes | · | 2 servings |

Dijon and dill give this salmon salad, made with canned fish, a more sophisticated taste. This dish makes a nice light lunch or dinner.

**ERIC'S OPTIONS**
If you like a smoky taste, try canned smoked salmon. It can be found at many specialty fish shops. Use the salmon salad in a sandwich.

| | | |
|---|---|---|
| 1 | 7 1/2-oz. (213-g) can salmon, drained well | 1 |
| 2 Tbsp. | light mayonnaise | 25 mL |
| 1 tsp. | Dijon mustard | 5 mL |
| 1 tsp. | chopped fresh dill | 5 mL |
| 1 | small celery rib, finely chopped | 1 |
| 1 | green onion, finely chopped | 1 |
| 2 Tbsp. | finely chopped red bell pepper | 25 mL |
| to taste | salt, pepper and lemon juice | to taste |
| 4 | butter or other cupped lettuce leaves | 4 |
| garnish | lemon wedges and dill sprigs | garnish |

Place the salmon, mayonnaise, mustard, dill, celery, green onion, bell pepper, salt, pepper and lemon juice in a bowl. Gently mix to combine. Place 2 lettuce leaves on each of 2 dinner plates. Spoon the salmon salad into the centre of the leaves. Garnish with lemon and dill.

# Chilled Baked Arctic Char
# with Fresh Coriander Sauce

preparation time · 20 minutes
cooking time · 12–15 minutes
makes · 4 servings

Fresh coriander, also called cilantro, adds a pleasing, pungent flavour and rich green colour to the sauce.

**ERIC'S OPTIONS**
Other fish fillets or steaks, such as tuna or salmon, can be used instead of Arctic char. The sauce also makes a nice dip for hot or cold cooked shrimp, crab and lobster.

| | | |
|---|---|---|
| 4 | 5-oz. (125-g) Arctic char fillets | 4 |
| 1/2 | lemon, juice of | 1/2 |
| 3 Tbsp. | olive oil | 45 mL |
| to taste | salt and white pepper | to taste |
| 1/4 cup | chopped fresh coriander, packed | 50 mL |
| 2 Tbsp. | mayonnaise | 25 mL |
| 2 Tbsp. | sour cream | 25 mL |
| 1 Tbsp. | white wine vinegar | 15 mL |
| pinch | cayenne pepper | pinch |
| garnish | lemon wedges and coriander sprigs | garnish |

Preheat the oven to 425°F (220°C). Place the fish in a single layer in a parchment-lined baking dish. Drizzle with the lemon juice and 1 Tbsp. (15 mL) of the olive oil; season with salt and pepper. Cover and bake for 12–15 minutes, or until just cooked through. Cool to room temperature, then wrap and refrigerate for at least 2 hours. Place the remaining oil, coriander, mayonnaise, sour cream, vinegar and cayenne pepper in a food processor or blender; pulse until a smooth sauce forms. Cover and refrigerate until well chilled. Place the fish on chilled dinner plates. Drizzle the sauce over top or serve it alongside. Garnish with lemon wedges and coriander sprigs.

# California Rolls

preparation time · 30–40 minutes
cooking time · 20 minutes
makes · 24 pieces

This straightforward recipe is designed for novice sushi makers wanting to learn the craft. The recipe can be expanded if you're feeding a larger group.

| THE RICE | | | |
|---|---|---|---|
| | 1³/4 cups | sushi rice | 425 mL |
| | 3 Tbsp. | rice vinegar | 45 mL |
| | 1¹/2 Tbsp. | sugar | 23 mL |
| | 1¹/2 tsp. | salt | 7 mL |
| | 2¹/2 cups | cold water | 625 mL |

| THE ROLLS | | | |
|---|---|---|---|
| | 3 | nori sheets | 3 |
| | 3 Tbsp. | mayonnaise | 45 mL |
| | ³/4 cup | crabmeat | 175 mL |
| | 1 | small, ripe, peeled avocado, cut into wedges | 1 |
| | | wasabi, soy sauce and pickled ginger | |

### THE RICE

Rinse the rice under cold running water, rubbing the grains together until the water runs clear. Cover the rice with cold water and soak for 30 minutes. While the rice is soaking, combine the vinegar, sugar and salt in a pot. Bring to a boil and stir to dissolve the sugar, about 30 seconds. Remove from the heat, cool to room temperature and set aside.

Drain the soaked rice well and place in a pot with the 2¹/2 cups (625 mL) cold water. Bring to a boil over high heat. Turn the heat to its lowest setting and cover the pot. Cook for 20 minutes, or until the rice is tender.

Spoon the rice into a large, shallow-sided pan, spreading it out in a thin layer to help it cool quickly. Stir in the vinegar mixture. When the rice has cooled to room temperature it is ready to use.

### THE ROLLS

Cover a sushi roller with plastic wrap. Place a sheet of nori on the plastic wrap. Moisten your hands with cold water, then spread 1/3 of the rice on the nori, leaving a 1-inch (2.5-cm) strip at the top of the nori. Spread a thin line of mayonnaise on the rice about 1/3 of the way up. Top with 1/3 of the crabmeat and avocado wedges. (If preparing the sushi rolls in advance, rub the avocado wedges with a little lemon juice to prevent them from browning.) Roll up the nori and filling in jelly-roll fashion, squeezing on the bamboo roller to compact the rice and filling as you go. Cut the roll into 8 pieces. Repeat with the remaining nori, rice and filling ingredients. Serve with wasabi for spicing up the sushi, soy sauce for dipping and pickled ginger for cleansing your palate.

### SHRIMP AND AVOCADO ROLLS

Replace the crabmeat with salad shrimp.

### SPICY TUNA ROLLS

Replace the crabmeat and avocado with a row of green onion and thin slices of raw tuna tossed with spicy Asian-style chili sauce.

### SALMON AND CUCUMBER ROLLS

Replace the crabmeat and avocado with a row of thinly cut cucumber strips and thin slices of raw salmon. For smoked salmon rolls, replace the raw salmon with smoked.

### NIGIRI SUSHI

Use the rice to make nigiri sushi (small pads of rice topped with seafood). Moisten your hands with cold water and shape the rice into 16-20 small oval pads. Top each with a dab of wasabi and then with thinly sliced raw or cooked seafood, such as salmon, smoked salmon, tuna, snapper or cooked and butterflied shrimp.

### HOW TO BUY, HANDLE AND PREPARE SEAFOOD FOR SUSHI

Ask a trusted fish retailer to recommend sushi-grade (very fresh) seafood. Salmon, tuna, scallops, squid and snapper are a few of the possibilities. Japanese food markets are a good source for sushi-grade fish, because they are most often sold already trimmed and ready to slice and use. Raw seafood used in sushi should be frozen for 48 hours before using. This process is designed to kill any potential parasites in the fish. Slice the seafood for sushi when it is still a bit frozen. The firmness will make it easier to get thin, even slices.

**NOTE**
Sushi rice, nori (seaweed sushi wrapper), wasabi and pickled ginger are available at most supermarkets and Japanese or Asian food stores. The sushi roller is a bamboo mat that can be found at Asian supply stores and well-stocked kitchenware stores.

**ERIC'S OPTIONS**
Use the same technique to make a range of other sushi rolls. (See left for some options.)

# Shellfish on Ice

| | | |
|---|---|---|
| preparation time | · | 30 minutes |
| cooking time | · | 2–3 minutes |
| makes | · | 4–6 servings |

Serve this dish on the hottest day of the summer, when you're looking for a delicious and decadent way to cool down. Make the dipping sauces in the morning so they will be ready to go once the seafood is prepared.

**ERIC'S OPTIONS**
Use 1 lb. (500 g) frozen cooked king crab or snow crab legs, thawed and cut into smaller pieces, instead of fresh crab.

| | | |
|---|---|---|
| 16–20 | large mussels | 16–20 |
| 1/3 cup | dry white wine | 75 mL |
| 1 | garlic clove, crushed | 1 |
| 2 | 1 1/4- to 1 1/2-lb. (625- to 750-g) cooked crabs, cleaned and separated into pieces (see How to Clean a Cooked Crab, page 121) | 2 |
| 16 | medium or large cooked and peeled shrimp | 16 |
| 12 | small oysters, shucked and left in the half shell (see page 17) | 12 |
| 1 recipe | Cocktail Sauce (see page 169) | 1 recipe |
| 1 recipe | Cool and Creamy Tarragon Sauce (see page 170) | 1 recipe |
| garnish | lemon wedges and dill or tarragon sprigs | garnish |

Wash the mussels in cold water and remove the beards. Place the wine and garlic in a pot and bring to a boil. Add the mussels, cover and cook until they just open. Drain the mussels well, spread them on a large tray and cool to room temperature. Remove the top shell from each mussel and discard. Set aside the meat-filled halves.

Fill a large tray or dish with sides with crushed ice. Arrange the mussels, crab, shrimp and oysters on top. Chill the seafood on the ice for 10–15 minutes. Place the sauces in bowls and nestle beside the seafood. Garnish with lemon wedges and dill or tarragon sprigs.

Tomato Soup with
Mussels and Fresh Basil   page 40

Chilled Crab
and Avocado Soup  page 44

Melon and Seafood
Salad with Mint and Cumin  page 48

Salad Niçoise   page 54

California Rolls   pages 62–63

Spaghetti with Anchovies, Cherry
Tomatoes and Italian Parsley  page 70

Fettuccini with Lobster, Saffron,
Peas and Oyster Mushrooms page 66

# PASTA&RICE

CHAPTER FOUR

# Fettuccini with Lobster, Saffron, Peas and Oyster Mushrooms

preparation time · 30 minutes
cooking time · 10 minutes
makes · 4 servings

This decadent pasta dish provides cost-effective luxury: one lobster feeds four people.

**ERIC'S OPTIONS**
Use 1/2 lb. (250 g) other cooked seafood, such as crabmeat, langoustines or salad shrimp, instead of the lobster. Any long pasta, such as linguini or spaghetti can be used instead of fettuccini.

| | | |
|---|---|---|
| 3/4 lb. | fettuccini | 375 g |
| 2 Tbsp. | olive oil | 25 mL |
| 2 | garlic cloves, finely chopped | 2 |
| 1/2 lb. | oyster mushrooms, sliced (lower stems removed and discarded) | 250 g |
| 1/2 cup | dry white wine | 125 mL |
| 1/2 tsp. | saffron | 2 mL |
| 1 Tbsp. | chopped fresh tarragon, or 1 tsp. (5 mL) dried | 15 mL |
| 2 cups | whipping cream | 500 mL |
| 1 1/2-lb. | cooked lobster, meat removed and thinly sliced | 750-g |
| 1/2 cup | frozen peas | 125 mL |
| to taste | salt and freshly cracked black pepper | to taste |
| 2 | green onions, finely chopped | 2 |

Cook the fettuccini in a large pot of boiling, lightly salted water until just tender. Meanwhile, heat the oil in a large skillet over medium-high heat. Add the garlic and mushrooms and cook until the mushrooms are just tender, about 3–4 minutes. Add the wine, saffron and tarragon and cook until the wine is reduced by half. Add the cream and cook until the sauce is slightly thickened. Add the lobster and peas and just heat through, about 2 minutes. Reduce the heat to medium-low.

When the pasta is cooked, drain well and mix it into the sauce. Season with salt and pepper. Divide among heated plates or pasta bowls and sprinkle each serving with green onions.

### TIPS FOR COOKING PASTA

The biggest mistake you can make when cooking pasta, whether it is skinny noodles or large shells, is not using enough water. If you use too little water, the starch that leaches out will cause the pasta to stick together. For every pound (500 g) of pasta, bring 12 cups (3 litres) of water to a boil. When it's boiling, add 1 Tbsp. (15 mL) of salt. Add the pasta and swirl to separate it. Once it comes back to a rapid boil, adjust the heat to a gentle boil. Cook until just tender; it should not be hard (undercooked), or mushy (overcooked). Cooking time will vary from brand to brand and shape to shape. For example, thick rigatoni may take 8–10 minutes to cook, while thin Asian-style egg noodles can be done in a minute or so. Check the package for the recommended cooking time.

# Whole-Wheat Penne with Tuna, Olives and Bell Peppers

preparation time · 25 minutes
cooking time · 8–10 minutes
makes · 4 servings

Whole-wheat pasta is high in fibre and rich in flavour, making this dish both healthy and tasty.

**ERIC'S OPTIONS**
If you like things spicy, add crushed chilis to taste when cooking the bell pepper and garlic. Try other fresh herbs, such as Italian parsley or oregano, or a combination of herbs, instead of, or along with, the basil.

| | | |
|---|---|---|
| 3/4 lb. | whole-wheat penne or other bite-sized pasta | 375 g |
| 2 Tbsp. | extra virgin olive oil, plus more for drizzling | 25 mL |
| 1 | medium red bell pepper, halved and thinly sliced | 1 |
| 1 | medium green bell pepper, halved and thinly sliced | 1 |
| 2 | garlic cloves, finely chopped | 2 |
| 1 | 6-oz. (170-g) can chunk tuna, drained and flaked | 1 |
| 1/3 cup | pitted black olives, coarsely chopped | 75 mL |
| 1 | lemon, juice and grated zest of | 1 |
| 1/4 cup | chopped fresh basil | 50 mL |
| to taste | salt and freshly cracked black pepper | to taste |

Cook the pasta in a large pot of boiling, lightly salted water until just tender. Meanwhile, heat the olive oil in a large skillet over medium heat. Add the red and green bell pepper and garlic and cook until just tender, about 3–4 minutes. Add the tuna, olives, lemon juice and zest and cook for 1 minute more. When the pasta is cooked, drain, saving 3/4 cup (175 mL) of the cooking liquid. Add the pasta and reserved cooking liquid, basil, salt and pepper to the tuna mixture. Gently toss to combine. Drizzle the servings with a little extra virgin olive oil, if desired.

# Linguini with Mussels
# in Tomato, Lemon and Parsley Sauce

| preparation time | · | 20 minutes |
| --- | --- | --- |
| cooking time | · | 15–18 minutes |
| makes | · | 4 servings |

Fresh mussels are a favourite seafood for three reasons: they're inexpensive, easy to cook and a joy to eat.

**ERIC'S OPTIONS**
Use fresh clams instead of mussels. Clams are more intense-tasting and the sauce will have a richer taste. The sauce can be made a day in advance. Cool to room temperature, then store in the fridge. Bring to a simmer before adding the mussels.

| | | |
| --- | --- | --- |
| 2 Tbsp. | olive oil | 25 mL |
| 1 | medium onion, finely chopped | 1 |
| 2–3 | garlic cloves, crushed | 2–3 |
| 1/2 cup | dry white wine | 125 mL |
| 1 | lemon, juice and grated zest of | 1 |
| 1 | 28-oz. (796-mL) can diced tomatoes | 1 |
| to taste | salt and freshly cracked black pepper | to taste |
| pinch | sugar | pinch |
| 3/4 lb. | linguini | 375 g |
| 2–2 1/2 lbs. | fresh mussels, washed and beards removed (see How to Clean a Mussel, page 27) | 1–1.25 kg |
| 1/4 cup | chopped fresh parsley | 50 mL |

Heat the oil in a large, wide pot over medium heat. Add the onion and garlic and cook until just tender, about 3–4 minutes. Add the wine, lemon juice and zest, tomatoes, salt, pepper and sugar. Bring to a simmer, cover loosely and cook for 10 minutes.

Meanwhile, bring a large pot of lightly salted water to a boil. Add the linguini and cook until just tender.

When the sauce has simmered for 10 minutes, add the mussels and half the parsley. Cover and cook until the mussels just open. Divide the linguini among heated pasta bowls. Spoon the mussels and sauce over the pasta and sprinkle with the remaining parsley.

# Spaghetti with Anchovies, Cherry Tomatoes and Italian Parsley

preparation time · 25–30 minutes
cooking time · 10–12 minutes
makes · 4 servings

A little bit of anchovy can add a large amount of flavour to a dish. Try this and you'll know what I mean.

**NOTE**

To make the bread crumbs, tear 1 to 2 (depending on size) slices of white bread into pieces and place in a food processor. Pulse to make coarse crumbs. Heat 1–2 Tbsp. (15–25 mL) of extra virgin olive oil over medium heat in a large non-stick skillet. Add the bread crumbs and cook, stirring, until lightly toasted and golden in colour.

| | | |
|---|---|---|
| 3/4 lb. | spaghetti | 375 g |
| 3 Tbsp. | extra virgin olive oil, plus more for drizzling | 45 mL |
| 1 | medium onion, finely chopped | 1 |
| 3 | garlic cloves, finely chopped | 3 |
| 4–6 | anchovy fillets, chopped | 4–6 |
| 1 | large green bell pepper, halved and thinly sliced | 1 |
| 18 | ripe cherry tomatoes, halved | 18 |
| 1/2 cup | dry white wine | 125 mL |
| 1/4 cup | chopped fresh Italian (flat-leaf) parsley | 50 mL |
| 1 cup | toasted bread crumbs | 250 mL |
| to taste | salt and freshly cracked pepper | to taste |

Bring a large pot of lightly salted water to a boil. Add the spaghetti and cook until just tender, about 8–10 minutes. Meanwhile, heat the olive oil in a large skillet over medium heat. Add the onion, garlic and anchovies and cook for 4–5 minutes. Add the bell pepper and cherry tomatoes and cook for 1–2 minutes more. Add the wine and continue cooking until it's reduced by half.

When the spaghetti is cooked, drain well, saving 3/4 cup (175 mL) of the cooking liquid. Add the spaghetti and the reserved cooking liquid, parsley, bread crumbs, salt and pepper to the skillet. Gently toss to combine. Drizzle each serving with a little extra virgin olive oil, if desired.

### ANCHOVIES 101

In some fish markets you can occasionally find fresh anchovies, which can be prepared similarly to fresh sardines or herring. Dried salted anchovies, which need to be soaked in several changes of cold water to soften them and reduce the saltiness, can also be found in some Mediterranean-style markets. The most common form of anchovies, however, and the style called for in most recipes, is fillets of the tiny fish salted and canned in oil.

The best anchovies will be packed in olive oil. To reduce the saltiness, rinse them thoroughly in cold water then dry on paper towels. Do not store leftover anchovies in the can. Place them in a tightly sealed jar, cover with olive oil and refrigerate for up to two months.

Anchovies are very strong-tasting and should be used in subtle ways—a rich hit of flavour that's not instantly recognizable. They are a cook's secret ingredient, something you can't put your finger on. Don't cover a pizza or a plate of antipasto with them unless you're crazy for the taste.

**ERIC'S OPTIONS**
Use 2–3 medium vine-ripened tomatoes, halved and chopped, instead of cherry tomatoes. For a milder or stronger anchovy taste, simply reduce or increase the amount used. If you do not want to use alcohol, replace the wine with chicken, fish or vegetable stock.

# Sensational Seafood Lasagna

preparation time · 40 minutes
cooking time · 55–60 minutes
makes · 8 servings

This lasagna is rich and decadent enough to serve on any special occasion. Serve it with a mixed green or Caesar salad.

**ERIC'S OPTIONS**
This lasagna can be made oven-ready several hours in advance. Cool to room temperature after assembling, and then wrap and refrigerate until ready to bake. Add 10 more minutes baking time, as you'll be starting it from cold. For even richer-tasting lasagna, replace the mozzarella cheese with a more complex-tasting Italian-style cheese, such as provolone or Asiago.

| | | |
|---|---|---|
| 2 1/2 cups | fish or chicken stock | 625 mL |
| 1 1/2 cups | light cream or milk | 375 mL |
| 2 | garlic cloves, finely chopped | 2 |
| 1/3 cup | all-purpose flour | 75 mL |
| to taste | salt and white pepper | to taste |
| pinch | ground nutmeg | pinch |
| 1/2 lb. | firm fish fillets, such as salmon or halibut, cut into small cubes | 250 g |
| 1 | 1-lb. (500-g) tub ricotta cheese | 1 |
| 2 | large eggs | 2 |
| 1/2 cup | chopped fresh basil | 125 mL |
| 1/2 lb. | cooked salad shrimp | 250 g |
| 1 cup | fresh or canned crabmeat, squeezed dry | 250 mL |
| 3/4–1 lb. | mozzarella cheese, grated | 375–500 g |
| 1/2 cup | freshly grated Parmesan cheese | 125 mL |
| 1 | 1-lb. (500-g) box lasagna noodles, cooked | 1 |
| to garnish | basil sprigs | to garnish |

Place 2 cups (500 mL) of the stock in a pot. Add the cream or milk and garlic, and bring to a simmer. Mix the remaining stock with the flour until smooth. Slowly whisk into the stock mixture. Bring back to a simmer and cook until the sauce thickens. Season with the salt, pepper and nutmeg; mix in the cubed fish. Remove from the heat and set aside. (The fish will cook through when baked in the lasagna.)

Combine the ricotta cheese with the eggs and basil. Season with salt and pepper and set aside. Preheat the oven to 350°F (180°F).

To assemble the lasagna, spoon a little sauce into the bottom of a 9- x 13-inch (3.5 L) casserole. Top with 4 noodles, 1/3 of the remaining sauce, and 1/2 of the shrimp and crab. Sprinkle with 1/3 of the mozzarella and Parmesan cheeses. Top with another layer of noodles and then with the ricotta cheese mixture. Top with another layer of noodles, another 1/3 of the sauce, the rest of the shrimp and crab and another 1/3 of the cheeses. Top with 4 more noodles and the remaining sauce and cheese. Bake, tented with foil so it does not touch the cheese, for 40 minutes. Uncover and bake for another 15–20 minutes, until brown and bubbly. Let the lasagna rest for 5–10 minutes before slicing and serving.

# Shrimp and Mixed Vegetable Chow Mein

| | | |
|---|---|---|
| preparation time | · | 25 minutes |
| cooking time | · | 5–6 minutes |
| makes | · | 4–6 servings |

To make this dish in a quick and efficient manner, have all your ingredients chopped and ready to go before you start cooking.

ERIC'S OPTIONS
Feel free to experiment and use different vegetables, such as chopped napa cabbage, broccoli florets or thinly sliced carrots.

| | | |
|---|---|---|
| 1 | 10 1/2-oz. (300-g) package fresh Chinese-style egg noodles | 1 |
| 1 Tbsp. | sesame oil | 15 mL |
| 2 Tbsp. | vegetable oil | 25 mL |
| 2 | garlic cloves, finely chopped | 2 |
| 1 Tbsp. | chopped fresh ginger | 15 mL |
| 1 | medium onion, cubed or sliced | 1 |
| 1 | medium red bell pepper, cubed or sliced | 1 |
| 3 | baby bok choy, trimmed and coarsely chopped | 3 |
| 1 | 14-oz. (398-mL) can baby corn, drained well | 1 |
| 1 | 8 oz. (228 mL) can sliced water chestnuts, drained well | 1 |
| 1/4 cup | light soy sauce | 50 mL |
| 1/2 cup | chicken or vegetable stock or water | 125 mL |
| to taste | Asian-style chili sauce | to taste |
| 24 | large cooked, peeled shrimp | 24 |
| 2 cups | bean sprouts | 500 mL |
| 2–3 | green onions, finely chopped | 2–3 |

Cook the noodles according to the package directions. Cool in cold water and drain well. Toss with the sesame oil and set aside.

Heat the vegetable oil in a wok or large skillet over high heat. Add the garlic and ginger and cook until fragrant, about 30 seconds. Add the onion, bell pepper, bok choy, corn and water chestnuts and stir-fry for 2–3 minutes. Add the soy sauce, stock or water and chili sauce, and bring to a simmer. Mix in the reserved noodles, shrimp and bean sprouts. Heat through. Spoon onto a heated platter, sprinkle with green onions and serve.

# Eric's Paella

preparation time · 40 minutes
cooking time · 45–50 minutes
makes · 6 servings

My version of paella has been developed over 20 years of making the dish. That said, this recipe changes each time, as I tend to base it on what looks good at the local supermarket or seafood store.

**ERIC'S OPTIONS**
Short-grain rice gives the risotto a slightly sticky, comforting mouth feel. However, a similar amount of long-grain rice can be substituted, if need be. Live lobster, cut and cleaned (see page 31) or cut and cleaned squid (see page 25) can be substituted for a portion of the seafood called for in the dish. Add them with the other seafood.

| | | |
|---|---|---|
| 9 | chicken wings, cut in half at the joint | 9 |
| 3 Tbsp. | olive oil | 45 mL |
| 1 tsp. | ground cumin | 5 mL |
| 1 tsp. | chili powder | 5 mL |
| to taste | salt and freshly cracked black pepper | to taste |
| 1 | medium onion, chopped | 1 |
| 1 | green bell pepper, chopped | 1 |
| 2 | garlic cloves, finely chopped | 2 |
| 1 | 28-oz. (796-mL) can diced tomatoes | 1 |
| 2 1/2 cups | short grain rice | 625 mL |
| 6 cups | chicken stock | 1.5 L |
| 2 tsp. | paprika | 10 mL |
| 1 tsp. | saffron threads, soaked in 2 Tbsp. (25 mL) boiling water | 5 mL |
| pinch | crushed chili flakes | pinch |
| 18 | large shrimp, peeled if desired | 18 |
| 18 | fresh mussels, washed and beards removed | 18 |
| 18 | fresh clams, rinsed in cold water | 18 |
| 3 | chorizo sausages, roasted or grilled and sliced | 3 |
| 1/2 cup | black olives, whole | 125 mL |
| | chopped parsley and lemon wedges | |

Preheat the oven to 375°F (190°C). Place the wing pieces in a bowl. Add 1 Tbsp. (15 mL) of the olive oil and the cumin, chili powder, salt and pepper. Toss to coat. Place the wings on a parchment-lined baking sheet. Bake for 25–30 minutes, or until cooked through. Remove from the oven and set aside.

Meanwhile, heat the remaining olive oil in a large, wide skillet or paella pan over medium heat. Add the onion, green pepper and garlic and cook until tender, about 3–4 minutes. Add the tomatoes, rice, stock, paprika, saffron and chili flakes. Season with salt and pepper and bring to a boil. Reduce the heat to medium-low and simmer gently for 20 minutes, until the rice is firm/tender and still slightly wet (add a little additional stock if necessary).

Place the reserved chicken wings, shrimp, mussels, clams, sausage and olives on top of the rice, gently pushing them down so they nestle into the rice. Cover and cook for 10 minutes, or until the prawns are cooked, the mussels and clams open, and the rice is tender. Sprinkle with parsley and top with lemon wedges. Place in the centre of the table and allow guests to help themselves.

# Candied Salmon on
# Mixed Vegetable Rice Bowl

preparation time · 25 minutes
cooking time · 20 minutes
makes · 4 servings

Brown sugar gives the salmon a heavenly glaze, while a touch of lemon in the rice balances its sweetness.

**ERIC'S OPTIONS**
The rice for this dish can be made up to a day in advance—something I do when I want to make a quick supper on a work day. After cooking, cool to room temperature and then store in the fridge until needed. When the salmon is halfway cooked, reheat the rice in the micro-wave or in a large skillet over medium heat. Add a little water to keep it moist.

|  |  |  |
|---|---|---|
| 1³/4 cups | long-grain rice | 425 mL |
| 3 cups | chicken or vegetable stock | 750 mL |
| 1 | lemon, juice and grated zest of | 1 |
| 1 | medium carrot, grated | 1 |
| 1/2 cup | frozen peas (do not thaw) | 125 mL |
| 1/2 cup | frozen corn kernels (do not thaw) | 125 mL |
| 3 | green onions, finely chopped | 3 |
| to taste | salt and freshly cracked black pepper | to taste |
| 4 | 5- to 6-oz. (150- to 175-g) salmon fillets or steaks | 4 |
| 2 Tbsp. | melted butter or olive oil | 25 mL |
| 1 Tbsp. | lemon juice | 15 mL |
| 1 Tbsp. | soy sauce | 15 mL |
| 3 Tbsp. | brown sugar | 45 mL |

Preheat the oven to 400°F (200°C). Rinse the rice under cold water to remove some of the outer starch. Drain well and place in a pot with the stock, lemon juice and zest, carrot, peas, corn, green onions (reserve some for garnish), salt and pepper. Bring to a boil, reduce the heat to its lowest setting, cover and cook until the rice is tender, about 20 minutes.

While the rice is cooking, place the salmon in a non-stick or parchment-lined baking dish. Brush with the butter or oil. Drizzle with lemon juice and soy sauce; season with salt and pepper and sprinkle with brown sugar. Bake 12–15 minutes, or until cooked through.

Divide the rice among 4 heated bowls. Top with a piece of salmon and drizzle any pan juices over top. Sprinkle with the reserved green onions.

# Risotto with Shrimp, Asparagus and Olives

preparation time · 40 minutes
cooking time · about 30 minutes
makes · 4 servings

To make a delicious supper, serve the risotto with warm crusty bread, a simple salad and a good, well-chilled bottle of white wine.

| THE RISOTTO | | | |
|---|---|---|---|
| 3 Tbsp. | butter or olive oil | 45 mL |
| 1 | medium onion, finely chopped | 1 |
| 1 1/2 cups | risotto rice, such as Arborio, Canaroli or Vialone Nano | 375 mL |
| 1/2 cup | dry white wine | 125 mL |
| 5–6 cups | hot fish, chicken or vegetable stock | 1.25–1.5 L |
| 2 Tbsp. | chopped Italian parsley | 25 mL |
| 1/2 cup | freshly grated Parmesan cheese | 125 mL |
| to taste | salt and freshly cracked black pepper | to taste |

| THE SHRIMP | | | |
|---|---|---|---|
| 2 Tbsp. | olive oil | 25 mL |
| 24 | medium shrimp, peeled, with tail portion intact | 24 |
| 8–10 | asparagus spears, trimmed, then sliced into 1-inch (2.5-cm) pieces | 8–10 |
| 1 | garlic clove, crushed | 1 |
| 1/4 cup | fish, chicken or vegetable stock | 50 mL |
| 1/2 cup | black olives, whole | 125 mL |
| to taste | salt and freshly cracked black pepper | to taste |
| 1 Tbsp. | chopped fresh parsley | 15 mL |

## THE RISOTTO

Heat the butter or olive oil in a large saucepan over medium heat. Add the onion and cook until tender, about 3–4 minutes. Add the rice and cook, stirring, until it achieves a nutty, slightly toasted aroma, about 3–4 minutes. Add the wine, adjust the heat so the mixture simmers gently, and cook until the wine is almost fully absorbed by the rice. Add 1 cup (250 mL) of the stock, stirring and cooking until it is almost fully absorbed by the rice. Add the remaining stock 1 cup (250 mL) at a time, cooking and stirring until the liquid is almost fully absorbed each time. You may not need all the stock. Stop adding stock when the rice is just tender and the liquid around it is supple and fluid, with a creamy, slightly soupy consistency. Stir in the parsley, Parmesan cheese, salt and pepper. Reserve on low heat until the shrimp are cooked.

## THE SHRIMP

Heat the oil in a large skillet over medium-high heat. Add the shrimp, asparagus and garlic and cook, stirring, for 2–3 minutes. Add the stock, olives, salt and pepper and cook for 1–2 minutes more, until the shrimp are just cooked.

To serve, spoon the risotto into heated bowls. Decorate the top with the shrimp, asparagus and olives. Sprinkle with parsley and a little more Parmesan cheese, if you like.

## ERIC'S OPTIONS

For a more budget-friendly risotto, use 1/2 lb. (250 g) of small, less expensive salad shrimp, instead of large shrimp. They don't require cooking, so add them to the skillet with the stock and olives, just heating them through.

# Rice Noodles with Bay Scallops and Green Thai Curry Sauce

preparation time · 5 minutes
cooking time · 15 minutes
makes · 4 servings

Creamy coconut milk and Thai-style flavourings, such as fiery green Thai curry paste, combine to make a quick and splendid sauce for noodles that any level of cook can create.

**NOTE**
Green Thai curry paste, coconut milk, fish sauce and rice noodles are available in the Asian food aisle of most supermarkets. Noodle package sizes vary. If what you purchased is larger than 1/2 lb. (250 g), use what you need and save the rest for another use.

**ERIC'S OPTIONS**
For spicier noodles, simply increase the amount of curry paste. If you're counting calories, use light coconut milk instead of regular. To substitute salad shrimp for the scallops, add them just before the noodles and cook only enough to heat them through.

| | | |
|---|---|---|
| 1 | 14-oz. (398-mL) can coconut milk | 1 |
| 1/2 cup | chicken, fish or vegetable stock | 125 mL |
| 2 tsp. | green Thai curry paste | 10 mL |
| 2 Tbsp. | fish sauce | 25 mL |
| 1 tsp. | brown sugar | 5 mL |
| 1 | lime, juice of | 1 |
| 1/2 lb. | bay or other small scallops | 250 g |
| 1/2 lb. | flat, Thai-style rice noodles | 250 g |
| 1/4 cup | chopped cilantro | 50 mL |
| to garnish | chopped green onion or cilantro, chopped shallots, lime wedges and chopped fresh chilies | to garnish |

Place the coconut milk, stock, curry paste, fish sauce, sugar and lime juice in a wok or large skillet. Bring to a gentle simmer and cook for 10 minutes. Meanwhile, bring a large pot of water to a boil.

Add the scallops to the coconut milk mixture and cook for 2–3 minutes, or until just cooked through, then lower the heat to medium-low. Add the noodles to the boiling water and cook for 1–2 minutes, or until just tender. Drain the noodles well, then add them and the cilantro to the skillet. Gently toss to combine. Divide the noodles among heated plates or bowls. Serve the garnishes in small bowls alongside for guests to flavour the noodles as they like.

# BURGERS, SEAFOOD CAKES & SANDWICHES

CHAPTER FIVE

# Cornmeal-Crusted Oyster Burgers

preparation time · 30 minutes
cooking time · 4 minutes
makes · 4 servings

Ice-cold beer pairs beautifully with these crispy oyster burgers flavoured with spicy mayonnaise.

**ERIC'S OPTIONS**
If you don't care for the slightly gritty crunch of cornmeal, just use bread crumbs. For a less spicy burger, spread the buns with store-bought or home-made tartar sauce (see page 171).

| | | |
|---|---|---|
| 1/2 cup | mayonnaise | 125 mL |
| 1 | lime, juice and zest of | 1 |
| 2–3 Tbsp. | chopped fresh cilantro | 25–45 mL |
| 1/2 tsp. | cayenne pepper, or to taste | 2 mL |
| 1/2 cup | cornmeal | 125 mL |
| 1/2 cup | bread crumbs | 125 mL |
| pinch | cayenne pepper | pinch |
| 1/2 tsp. | salt | 2 mL |
| 1/2 tsp. | black pepper | 2 mL |
| 1 cup | all-purpose flour | 250 mL |
| 2 | large eggs, beaten and mixed with 1/4 cup (50 mL) milk | 2 |
| 12 | medium shucked oysters, about two 1/2-lb. (250-mL) tubs | 12 |
| | vegetable oil | |
| 4 | large burger buns, warmed | 4 |
| 4 | lettuce leaves | 4 |
| to serve | sliced tomato and onion | to serve |

Combine the mayonnaise, lime juice and zest, cilantro and 1/2 tsp. (2 mL) cayenne pepper in a bowl. Cover and keep in the fridge until the oysters are cooked.

Combine the cornmeal, bread crumbs, pinch of cayenne pepper, salt and black pepper in a wide, shallow dish. Place the flour in another dish, and the egg mixture in a third dish.

Drain the oysters well. Coat them first in flour, shaking off the excess. Dip in the egg mixture, making sure they are evenly coated. Set in the cornmeal mixture, gently pressing it onto the oysters.

Heat 1/8 inch (3 mm) of vegetable oil in a large skillet over medium-high heat. Fry the oysters for 2 minutes per side, until crispy, golden and just cooked through. If you are cooking in batches, keep the cooked oysters warm in a 200°F (95°C) oven.

Spread the mayonnaise mixture on the burger buns. Place a lettuce leaf on the bottom of each bun. Top with 3 fried oysters and some tomato and onion slices. Serve immediately.

# Tex-Mex
# Salmon Burgers

preparation time · 15 minutes
cooking time · 6–8 minutes
makes · 4 servings

Rich-tasting salmon pairs well with bold and complex flavours like the spices found in this colourful burger.

**ERIC'S OPTIONS**
Substitute other firm fish fillets, such as halibut or tuna, for the salmon. For added spice, top the fish with thin slices of fresh or canned jalapeño peppers just before serving.

| | | |
|---|---|---|
| 4 | 1/4-lb. (125-g) salmon fillets | 4 |
| 2 Tbsp. | olive oil | 25 mL |
| 1 tsp. | chili powder | 5 mL |
| 1 tsp. | ground cumin | 5 mL |
| 1/4 tsp. | cayenne pepper | 1 mL |
| 1/2 tsp. | dried oregano | 2 mL |
| to taste | salt and freshly cracked black pepper | to taste |
| 4 | kaiser buns, cut in half | 4 |
| 1/4 cup | mayonnaise | 50 mL |
| 4 | lettuce leaves | 4 |
| 1/2 cup | tomato salsa, store-bought or homemade | 125 mL |
| 1 | small, ripe avocado, peeled and sliced into thin wedges | 1 |
| 1 | lime, juice of | 1 |

Brush the salmon with the olive oil; sprinkle with chili powder, cumin, cayenne pepper, oregano, salt and pepper. Cover and let the salmon marinate at room temperature for 20 minutes.

Preheat a non-stick or lightly oiled grill to medium-high. Grill the salmon for 3–4 minutes per side, or until just cooked through. Spread the buns with the mayonnaise and top with lettuce. Add the salmon and top with a spoonful of the salsa and a few wedges of avocado. Drizzle with lime juice, set on top of the bun and serve.

### REMOVING SALMON PIN BONES

Unless your seafood retailer has removed them, salmon fillets have small pin bones embedded in the flesh. To remove them before cooking, lay the fillet on a work surface and run your finger down the upper middle of the flesh. The bones should pop up. Grab the end of the bones with tweezers or needle-nose pliers, then tug to pull them out. If you want to avoid this task, buy tail-end fillet portions, which have no pin bones.

# Shrimp Cakes with Chipotle Tartar Sauce

preparation time · 20 minutes
cooking time · 6–8 minutes
makes · 4 servings

These small, moist cakes and the spicy sauce are a tasty way to kick off dinner. Accompanied by a side salad, they make a fine meal all on their own.

| THE SAUCE | | | |
|---|---|---|---|
| 1 | chipotle pepper, very finely chopped | 1 |
| 1/2 cup | mayonnaise | 125 mL |
| 2 | green onions, finely chopped | 2 |
| 1/4 cup | finely chopped sweet mixed pickles | 50 mL |
| 2 | green onions, finely chopped | 2 |
| to taste | salt and lime juice | to taste |

| THE SHRIMP CAKES | | | |
|---|---|---|---|
| 10 oz. | cooked salad shrimp | 300 g |
| 1 | large egg, beaten | 1 |
| 2 Tbsp. | all-purpose flour | 25 mL |
| 1/3 cup | mayonnaise | 75 mL |
| 2 | green onions, finely chopped | 2 |
| 2 Tbsp. | chopped fresh cilantro or parsley | 25 mL |
| to taste | salt, lime juice and hot pepper sauce | to taste |
| 1 cup | crushed cracker or bread crumbs | 250 mL |
| 3 Tbsp. | vegetable oil | 45 mL |
| garnish | lime wedges and cilantro or parsley sprigs | garnish |

### THE SAUCE
Combine the sauce ingredients in a small bowl. Cover and refrigerate until needed.

### THE SHRIMP CAKES
Line a tray with plastic wrap or parchment paper. Place the shrimp on a cutting board and chop almost to a mince, or pulse in a food processor to achieve this consistency. Transfer the shrimp to a bowl. Add the egg, flour, mayonnaise, green onion, cilantro or parsley, salt, lime juice and hot pepper sauce. Mix well to combine. (The mixture will appear quite wet.) Place the crumbs in a wide, shallow dish. Moisten your hands lightly with cold water and shape 1/4 cup (50 mL) of the shrimp mixture into a ball. Set it on the crumbs and sprinkle the top and sides with crumbs. Gently form into a cake about 3 inches (8 cm) wide and 1/2 inch (1 cm) thick. Place on the prepared tray. Repeat with the remaining shrimp mixture. You should get 8 shrimp cakes.

Heat the oil in a large, non-stick skillet or griddle over medium heat. Cook the shrimp cakes for 3–4 minutes per side. Divide the cakes among 4 plates. Place a spoonful of chipotle tartar sauce alongside and garnish with a lime wedge and a sprig of cilantro or parsley.

### NOTE
Chipotle peppers, which are actually smoked jalapeño peppers, are sold in cans in the Mexican food section of most supermarkets. Leftover chipotle peppers can be stored in a tightly sealed jar in the refrigerator for several weeks. Use them in dishes such as chili, stews, barbecue sauces and taco fillings.

**ERIC'S OPTIONS**
For a crisper crust, replace 1/2 cup (125 mL) of the bread or cracker crumbs with cornmeal. To make crab cakes, replace the shrimp with 10 oz. (300 g) of cooked and well-drained crabmeat.

# Thai-Style Fish Cakes

preparation time · 15 minutes
cooking time · 6–8 minutes
makes · 4 servings

Serve these cakes with steamed rice and stir-fried vegetables.

**ERIC'S OPTIONS**
To make Thai-style shrimp cakes, replace the fish with 1 lb. (500 g) of raw, peeled shrimp and proceed as directed.

|  |  |  |
|---|---|---|
| 1 lb. | boneless white fish fillets, such as sole, cod, snapper or halibut | 500 g |
| 3 | green onions, finely chopped | 3 |
| 1/4 cup | chopped cilantro | 50 mL |
| 1 | lime, grated zest and juice of | 1 |
| 2 | garlic cloves, chopped | 2 |
| 2 tsp. | Asian-style hot chili sauce or to taste | 10 mL |
| 2 tsp. | chopped fresh ginger | 10 mL |
| 2 tsp. | fish sauce | 10 mL |
| 1 | large egg, lightly beaten | 1 |
| 1/4 cup | cornstarch | 50 mL |
| 3 Tbsp. | vegetable oil | 45 mL |
| garnish | lime wedges | garnish |
| | Asian-style sweet chili sauce for dipping | |

Place the fish fillets, green onion, cilantro, lime zest and juice, garlic, hot chili sauce, ginger, fish sauce, and egg in a food processor. Pulse until coarsely chopped. (Do not overmix to a paste. If you don't have a food processor, finely chop all the ingredients and combine in a bowl.) Transfer the mixture to a bowl. Cover and refrigerate for 1 hour to allow the flavours to meld.

Line a tray with plastic wrap or parchment paper. Dust your hands with a little cornstarch, then shape 1/4-cup (50-mL) amounts of the mixture into small, 1/2-inch-thick (1-cm) patties and set on the tray.

Heat the oil in a large skillet over medium to medium-high heat. Coat the cakes with a little cornstarch and fry for 3–4 minutes per side, until golden brown and cooked through. Garnish with lime wedges and serve sweet chili sauce alongside for dipping.

**NOTE**
Fish sauce and Asian-style hot and sweet chili sauces are sold in the Asian food aisle of most supermarkets and at Asian markets.

# Smoked Cod Cakes with Dill Mayonnaise

preparation time · 20 minutes
cooking time · 10 minutes
makes · 4 servings

These savoury cakes make a nice maritime-style dinner when served with boiled or steamed and buttered vegetables, such as cabbage, carrots and green beans.

| THE MAYONNAISE | 1/2 cup | light mayonnaise | 125 mL |
|---|---|---|---|
| | 1 tsp. | Dijon mustard | 5 mL |
| | 2 tsp. | chopped fresh dill | 10 mL |
| | 2 tsp. | horseradish | 10 mL |
| | to taste | salt and white pepper | to taste |
| THE FISH CAKES | 3/4 lb. | smoked cod | 375 g |
| | 2 | medium baking potatoes, peeled, boiled and mashed | 2 |
| | 2 | green onions, finely chopped | 2 |
| | 1 Tbsp. | chopped fresh dill | 15 mL |
| | 1 | garlic clove, crushed | 1 |
| | 1 | large egg, beaten | 1 |
| | to taste | salt and white pepper | to taste |
| | 1 cup | bread crumbs | 250 mL |
| | 3 Tbsp. | vegetable oil | 45 mL |
| | to garnish | lemon wedges and dill sprigs | to garnish |

### THE SAUCE

Combine all the ingredients in a bowl. Cover and refrigerate until the cakes are cooked.

### THE FISH CAKES

Remove and discard any skin from the cod. Break the fish into small flakes, removing any bones. Place the flaked cod in a bowl. Add the mashed potatoes, green onions, dill, garlic, egg, salt and pepper. Mix well to combine. Moisten your hands with cold water and form the mixture into 4 cakes about 3/4 inch (2 cm) thick. Coat the cakes in the bread crumbs, pressing them on gently. Heat the oil in a large skillet set over medium to medium-high heat. Fry the cakes for 3–4 minutes per side, until golden brown and heated through. Serve with a dollop of the mayonnaise alongside; garnish with lemon wedges and dill sprigs.

### ERIC'S OPTIONS

To make smoked salmon cakes, replace the cod with an equal amount of hot-smoked salmon and proceed as directed (see Cold- and Hot-Smoked Salmon, page 21). For a savoury brunch, top the cakes with poached eggs and omit the mayonnaise.

# Italian-Style Fish Burgers

preparation time · 10 minutes
cooking time · 8 minutes
makes · 4 servings

Olive oil, oregano, mozzarella and tomato give these fish burgers a pleasing taste of Italy.

**ERIC'S OPTIONS**
Instead of grilling the fish, pan-fry for a similar length of time in a non-stick skillet over medium-high heat. Finish as described in the recipe.

| | | |
|---|---|---|
| 4 | 1/4-lb. (125-g) boneless, skinless, fillets of halibut or other firm fish | 4 |
| 2 Tbsp. | olive oil | 25 mL |
| 1/2 tsp. | paprika | 2 mL |
| 1 tsp. | dried oregano | 5 mL |
| to taste | salt and freshly cracked black pepper | to taste |
| 1 1/4 cups | tomato-based pasta sauce, heated | 300 mL |
| 4 | slices mozzarella cheese | 4 |
| 4 | panini or hamburger buns, warmed | 4 |
| 4 | lettuce leaves | 4 |

Preheat the grill to medium-high. Brush the fish fillets with the olive oil; sprinkle with the paprika, oregano, salt and pepper. Grill for 2–3 minutes per side. Top each piece of fish with a spoonful of the pasta sauce and a slice of mozzarella cheese. When the cheese is melted and the fish is cooked through, cut the panini or hamburger buns in half. Place a lettuce leaf on the bottom of each bun, top with a piece of halibut and set on the top halves of the buns. Serve the remaining pasta sauce in a small bowl alongside for dipping the burgers in.

# Mediterranean-Style Tuna Wrap

preparation time · 10 minutes
cooking time · none
makes · 2 servings

Pack these tasty wraps for a summer picnic or workday lunch.

**NOTE**
Warming the tortilla shells slightly in the microwave before filling makes them more flexible and easier to roll.

**ERIC'S OPTIONS**
Use flavoured tortilla shells such as tomato, spinach or herb instead of plain. Use pitted green olives instead of black. For a more intense tomato taste, replace the fresh tomato with 1/3 cup (75 mL) or so of chopped sun-dried tomatoes.

| | | |
|---|---|---|
| 2 Tbsp. | mayonnaise | 25 mL |
| 2 Tbsp. | pesto | 25 mL |
| 2 | 10-inch (25-cm) tortillas | 2 |
| 1 | 6-oz. (170-g) can chunk tuna, drained well and flaked | 1 |
| 1 | medium ripe tomato, finely chopped | 1 |
| 1 cup | shredded lettuce | 250 mL |
| 1/4 cup | pitted black olives, coarsely chopped | 50 mL |
| 1/4 cup | crumbled feta cheese | 50 mL |
| to taste | salt and freshly cracked black pepper | to taste |

Combine the mayonnaise and pesto in a small bowl. Spread the mixture on one side of each tortilla. Arrange the tuna, tomato and lettuce in a row in the centre of each tortilla, leaving about 1 1/2 inches (4 cm) free at each side. Sprinkle the olives and feta cheese over top and season with salt and pepper. Fold over the sides of the tortilla and then roll it up tightly into a closed cylinder. Slice in half at a slight angle before serving.

# Crab, Black Bean
## and Monterey Jack Quesadillas

preparation time · 20 minutes
cooking time · 4–6 minutes
makes · 4 appetizer servings; or 2 main courses

Serve these quesadillas as an appetizer with sour cream, guacamole and salsa for dipping. Or serve them with Spanish-style rice or a green salad for a main course.

**ERIC'S OPTIONS**
Use 1 cup (250 mL) of salad shrimp instead of crab.
To spice up these quesadillas, add 1 small jalapeño pepper, finely chopped, to the filling mixture.

| | | |
|---|---|---|
| 1 cup | crabmeat | 250 mL |
| 1 | 19-oz. (540-mL) can black beans, drained well | 1 |
| 1 | medium red or yellow bell pepper, finely chopped | 1 |
| 1/4 cup | cilantro or finely chopped green onions | 50 mL |
| 1 tsp. | chili powder | 5 mL |
| 1 tsp. | ground cumin | 5 mL |
| 2 cups | grated Monterey Jack cheese | 500 mL |
| 4 | 10-inch (25-cm) tortilla shells | 4 |
| 2–3 Tbsp. | vegetable oil | 25–45 mL |

Place the crabmeat, beans, bell pepper, cilantro or green onion, chili powder, cumin and cheese in a bowl. Gently mix to combine. Divide the mixture evenly between the tortillas, placing it on one half of the tortilla. Fold the other half over to cover the filling and gently press the tortilla together. Heat the oil in a non-stick skillet or griddle set over medium heat. When the oil is hot, add the quesadillas and cook for 2–3 minutes per side, or until they are golden brown and the cheese is melted. Remove and place on a cutting board. Cool slightly to allow the cheese to set before cutting the quesadillas into wedges.

# Lobster
# Rolls

preparation time · 25 minutes
cooking time · none
makes · 4 servings

A seafood book would not be complete without a recipe for this popular east coast sandwich. Here's my version of it.

**ERIC'S OPTIONS**
Use crusty buns or small croissants instead of hot dog buns. Spice up the lobster mixture by mixing in curry powder to taste.

| | | |
|---|---|---|
| 1 | 1¹/₂-lb. (750-g) cooked lobster | 1 |
| 1 | celery rib, finely chopped | 1 |
| 2 | green onions, finely chopped | 2 |
| ¹/₂ cup | mayonnaise | 125 mL |
| 1 Tbsp. | lemon juice | 15 mL |
| to taste | salt and white pepper | to taste |
| pinch | cayenne pepper | pinch |
| 4 | hot dog buns | 4 |
| 1 cup | thinly sliced head or leaf lettuce | 250 mL |

Remove the meat from the lobster and cut into small pieces. Place in a bowl and mix in the celery, green onion, mayonnaise and lemon juice. Season with salt, white pepper and cayenne. Line the hot dog buns with shredded lettuce. Stuff in the lobster mixture and serve.

# ONTHE STOVETOP

CHAPTER SIX

# Lemon
## Pepper Snapper

preparation time · 20 minutes
cooking time · 6–8 minutes
makes · 4 servings

I love the combination of tart lemon and spicy black pepper. In this dish they combine to accent and lift the flavour of the mild-tasting fish.

**ERIC'S OPTIONS**
For an added flavour boost, serve the snapper with homemade Tartar Sauce (see page 171). For a crunchier crust, replace half the bread crumbs with cornmeal. Other fish fillets, such as sole, flounder or salmon, can be used in place of the snapper.

| | | |
|---|---|---|
| 1 cup | bread crumbs | 250 mL |
| 1 | lemon, grated zest of | 1 |
| 2 tsp. | cracked black pepper | 10 mL |
| 1/2 tsp. | salt | 2 mL |
| 1/2 cup | all-purpose flour | 125 mL |
| 2 | large eggs, beaten with 1/4 cup (50 mL) milk | 2 |
| 4 | 5- to 6-oz. (150- to 175-g) snapper fillets | 4 |
| 3 Tbsp. | vegetable oil | 45 mL |

Combine the bread crumbs with the lemon zest, pepper and salt in a shallow dish. Place the flour in a second shallow dish and the egg mixture in a third. Coat the snapper in flour, shaking off any excess. Dip the snapper in the egg mixture, making sure it is evenly coated. Set the fillets in the crumb mixture and coat both sides, gently pressing the crumbs on.

Heat the oil in a large non-stick skillet set over medium to medium-high heat. Add the fish and cook for 3–4 minutes per side, or until nicely coloured and cooked through.

BUYING AND HANDLING FRESH SEAFOOD

Fresh seafood should smell sweet and sea-like. If it smells "fishy," it is past its prime and should be avoided. If you're too shy to smell what you hope to buy, ask your retailer when it came in. A reputable fishmonger will let you know which catch is the freshest.

You can also check seafood visually for freshness. Fresh fish will have firm flesh that glistens; it should not look dull, soft or look like it's falling apart. Shrimp should have bright-looking shells and look full, not shrivelled. The shells of oysters, clams or mussels should be shut tight, or should shut tight when gently tapped. If they don't shut they are dead and should not be eaten. Live lobster, crab and fish should struggle vigorously when pulled from their holding tanks. If they are slow-moving, don't buy them.

Live seafood should be purchased the day you intend to cook it. Do not cook if it's dead. Seafood such as lobster and crab deteriorate quickly and may not be safe to eat. Other seafood is also best cooked the day you purchase it, but, if need be, it can be stored in the coldest part of your fridge for one day. Remove from its packaging and place in a covered container. To keep it super-chilled, set the container on a bowl of crushed ice.

# Pan-Fried Halibut
# with Lemon Chive Butter

preparation time · 5 minutes
cooking time · 6–8 minutes
makes · 2 servings

A quick-cooking dish with minimal ingredients, this accents the fine flavour of halibut, rather than masking it.

ERIC'S OPTIONS
If fresh chives are unavailable, replace with 1 finely chopped green onion. For a different lemon/herb taste, use 1 Tbsp. (15 mL) of chopped fresh tarragon, oregano or basil.

| | | |
|---|---|---|
| 2 Tbsp. | olive oil | 25 mL |
| 2 | 5-oz. (150-g) halibut fillets | 2 |
| to taste | salt and white pepper | to taste |
| 2 Tbsp. | melted butter | 25 mL |
| 1/2 | lemon, juice of | 1/2 |
| 1 Tbsp. | chopped fresh chives | 15 mL |

Place the olive oil in a non-stick skillet over medium-high heat. Season the halibut with salt and pepper and cook for 3–4 minutes per side (a little longer if the fillets are thick), or until cooked through. Divide the fish between 2 heated dinner plates.

Drain the oil from the pan, and then add the butter, lemon juice and chives. Cook and stir until the butter just melts. Pour the butter over the fish and serve.

### HOW TO FREEZE AND THAW FISH

If fresh fish is on special you may wish to take advantage of the price and freeze some for later use. Freeze as soon after purchasing as possible. Rinse whole fish, fillets or steaks under cold water and pat them dry with paper towels. Wrap in plastic wrap, wrapping fillets and steaks individually, and squeezing out all the air. Wrap again in aluminum foil. This double protection will prevent oxidation and freezer burn.

Write the contents and date on a freezer label. To keep fish fillets and steaks flat, freeze them solid on a tray; when frozen solid, remove and store in the desired spot in the freezer. Fish will keep in the freezer for 1 to 2 months.

To use, thaw fillets or steaks overnight in the refrigerator, not out on the counter. Whole fish can take up to 24 hours to thaw, depending on the size. Cook soon after thawing.

# Deviled Skate with Lemon Parsley Mayonnaise

| preparation time | · | 20 minutes |
| cooking time | · | 6–8 minutes |
| makes | · | 4 servings |

Skate wings come in various sizes. If you're uncomfortable cutting them into portions, ask your fish retailer to do it for you.

| THE MAYONNAISE | 1/4 cup | mayonnaise | 50 mL |
|---|---|---|---|
| | 2 Tbsp. | chopped fresh parsley | 25 mL |
| | 1/2 | lemon, juice of, or to taste | 1/2 |
| | to taste | salt and white pepper | to taste |
| THE SKATE | 3/4 cup | bread crumbs | 175 mL |
| | 1 Tbsp. | chopped fresh parsley | 15 mL |
| | 1 1/2 lbs. | skinless skate wings, cut into 4 portions | 750 g |
| | to taste | salt and white pepper | to taste |
| | 2 Tbsp. | Dijon mustard | 25 mL |
| | 2 Tbsp. | olive oil | 25 mL |
| | 1 Tbsp. | butter | 15 mL |
| | garnish | lemon wedges and parsley sprigs | garnish |

### THE MAYONNAISE
Combine all the ingredients in a bowl. Cover and refrigerate until needed.

### THE SKATE
Combine the bread crumbs and parsley in a shallow dish. Rinse the skate in cold water and pat dry. Season the skate with salt and white pepper. Brush both sides with mustard. Coat the skate in the bread crumb mixture, gently pressing the crumbs on.

Heat the oil and butter in a large non-stick skillet over medium to medium-high heat. Add the skate and cook for 3–4 minutes on each side, or until golden brown and cooked through. Arrange the fish, rib-like side down, on 4 plates. Place a dollop of the mayonnaise alongside the fish, garnish with lemon and parsley and serve.

### WHAT IS SKATE?
Skate, also called a ray, is member of the family Rajidae, which is closely related to sharks. The term skate is most often applied to members of the species that are used for eating, while ray generally refers to sport fish, such as electric ray and giant manta ray.

The wing-like pectoral fins, which propel the fish along the ocean floor, are the edible part of a skate. They are generally sold with their tough skin removed and feature a flesh that's firm, white and sweet, with a taste some say is similar to scallop.

What scares some people away from trying skate is the rib-like, gelatinous cartilage found below the flesh. But don't worry, the flesh slides away from it very easily once cooked.

Some say that, like shark meat, skate must be soaked in acidulated water, such as lemon juice, to remove its natural ammonia odour. I suggest a simple rinse in cold water and a pat dry unless the fish does have a strong odour of ammonia. Skate can be cooked in a variety of ways, including frying, baking and poaching.

### ERIC'S OPTIONS
The mustard/crumb coating can be used on other similar-sized fish fillets, such as monkfish, cod, snapper and halibut.

# Southern-Style
# Fish Fry

preparation time · 20 minutes
cooking time · 6–8 minutes
makes · 4 servings

I learned to dip fish in water, rather than beaten egg, during a trip to the southern U.S. The chef in a Cajun restaurant I visited said it helps create a crispier crust. He was right. Try this dish when you're camping and need a simple but tasty way to fry up your fish.

**NOTE**
Cajun spice, a Southern-style spice blend, is sold at most supermarkets and bulk food stores.

**ERIC'S OPTIONS**
Try serving the fish with chipotle tartar sauce (see Shrimp Cakes with Chipotle Tartar Sauce, page 89).

| | | |
|---|---|---|
| 1 cup | bread or cracker crumbs | 250 mL |
| 1–2 Tbsp. | Cajun spice | 15–25 mL |
| 4 | 5-oz. (150-g) fish fillets, such as snapper, salmon or sole | 4 |
| 1/2 cup | all-purpose flour | 125 mL |
| 3 Tbsp. | vegetable oil | 45 mL |

Combine the crumbs and Cajun spice in a shallow dish. Fill another shallow dish with 1/2 inch (1 cm) cold water. Coat the fish fillets in flour, shaking off the excess. Quickly dip in the water just until moistened on both sides. Set the fillets in the crumb mixture and coat on both sides, gently pressing the crumbs on. Transfer to a plate. Heat the oil in a large skillet over medium to medium-high heat. Cook the fish fillets for 3–4 minutes per side, depending on the thickness, until nicely coloured and cooked through.

# Green Thai Curry Shrimp

preparation time · 10 minutes
cooking time · 10 minutes
makes · 4 servings

Creamy coconut milk, hot green Thai curry paste and tart lime juice are a few of the ingredients that make this spicy shrimp dish addictive.

**NOTE**
Green Thai curry paste is sold at most supermarkets and Asian food markets.

**ERIC'S OPTIONS**
To make this dish more or less spicy, simply increase or decrease the amount of green Thai curry paste. Try using large scallops or 1-inch (2.5-cm) cubes of salmon fillet instead of shrimp. Cooking time will be about the same.

| | | |
|---|---|---|
| 1 | 14-oz. (398-mL) can coconut milk | 1 |
| 1 Tbsp. | chopped fresh ginger | 15 mL |
| 2 | garlic cloves, chopped | 2 |
| 2 | limes, juice of | 2 |
| 3 Tbsp. | brown sugar, packed | 45 mL |
| 2 tsp. | green Thai curry paste | 10 mL |
| 24 | large shrimp, peeled, with tail portion left intact | 24 |
| 1/4 cup | chopped fresh cilantro | 50 mL |
| to taste | salt | to taste |

Place the coconut milk, ginger, garlic, lime juice, brown sugar and curry paste in a pot and bring to a simmer over medium heat. Gently simmer for 5 minutes, stirring occasionally. Add the shrimp and cook for 3–4 minutes, or until cooked through. Stir in the cilantro and salt and serve.

# Pan-Seared Scallops on Ginger-Spiked Mango Sauce

preparation time · 10 minutes
cooking time · 10 minutes
makes · 4 servings

Scallops taste almost sweet and pair well with tropical flavours. This combination of mango, lime and ginger brings one of my favourite molluscs to delicious new heights. Serve with steamed rice and stir-fried vegetables.

| THE MANGO SAUCE | 1 | medium, ripe mango, peeled and coarsely chopped | 1 |
|---|---|---|---|
| | 2 tsp. | freshly grated ginger | 10 mL |
| | 2 Tbsp. | fresh lime juice | 25 mL |
| | 2 tsp. | brown sugar, or to taste | 10 mL |
| | pinch | crushed chili flakes | pinch |
| | 1/4 cup | water | 50 mL |
| THE SCALLOPS | 20 | large sea scallops | 20 |
| | 1 tsp. | ground cumin | 5 mL |
| | to taste | salt and white pepper | to taste |
| | 2 Tbsp. | olive oil | 25 mL |
| | 2 Tbsp. | fresh lime juice | 25 mL |
| | 4 | cilantro sprigs and lime slices for garnish | 4 |

### THE MANGO SAUCE

Place all the ingredients in a food processor or blender and purée until smooth. Transfer to a small pot and gently simmer over medium heat for 10 minutes. Keep warm over low heat until the scallops are cooked.

### THE SCALLOPS

Season the scallops with the cumin, salt and pepper. Heat the oil in a non-stick skillet over high heat. Cook the scallops for 1–2 minutes per side, or until just cooked through. Sprinkle with lime juice and remove from the heat. Spoon the mango sauce on 4 plates. Arrange the scallops on top. Garnish with cilantro and lime.

### ERIC'S OPTIONS

For curried mango sauce, omit the crushed chili flakes from the sauce and add curry paste or powder to taste before simmering the sauce.

# Sizzling Seafood Stir-Fry

| preparation time | · | 20 minutes |
| cooking time | · | 6–8 minutes |
| makes | · | 4 servings |

Have all the ingredients chopped and ready to go before whipping up this quick stir-fry.

ERIC'S OPTIONS
For a sweeter, less salty, taste use hoisin sauce instead of oyster sauce.
For a spicy stir-fry, add Asian-style hot chili sauce to taste when adding the oyster sauce.

| | | |
|---|---|---|
| 1/4 cup | oyster sauce | 50 mL |
| 2 Tbsp. | light soy sauce | 25 mL |
| 1 tsp. | honey | 5 mL |
| 2 tsp. | sesame oil | 10 mL |
| 1 Tbsp. | rice vinegar | 15 mL |
| 2 | green onions, finely chopped | 2 |
| 2 Tbsp. | vegetable oil | 25 mL |
| 2 | garlic cloves, finely chopped | 2 |
| 2 tsp. | chopped fresh ginger | 10 mL |
| 8 | medium to large shrimp, peeled and cut in half lengthwise | 8 |
| 8 | large scallops, cut in half lengthwise | 8 |
| 1/2 lb. | firm fish fillet, such as salmon, swordfish or halibut, cubed | 250 g |
| 4 | heads baby bok choy, trimmed and separated into leaves | 4 |
| 1 | medium yellow or red bell pepper, cut into small cubes | 1 |
| to taste | freshly cracked black pepper | to taste |

In a bowl, combine the oyster sauce, soy sauce, honey, sesame oil, rice vinegar and green onions.

Heat the oil in a wok or large skillet over medium-high heat. Add the garlic and ginger and stir-fry for 30 seconds. Add the shrimp, scallops and cubed fish and cook for 3–4 minutes, or until just cooked through. Transfer the seafood to a plate. Add the baby bok choy and bell pepper to the pan and stir-fry for 2 minutes. Add the oyster sauce mixture and $1/4$ cup (50 mL) of cold water and bring to a simmer. Return the seafood to the pan and cook until just heated through. Season with pepper and serve.

# Shrimp and Scallop Newburg

preparation time · 20 minutes
cooking time · 15 minutes
makes · 4 servings

Serve this divinely rich seafood dish on a special occasion, when you need a dish that will impress, but is simple enough not to leave you stressed.

**ERIC'S OPTIONS**
If you don't have sherry, substitute white or sparkling wine. If you don't want to use alcohol, simply replace the sherry with stock. For an even more decadent Newburg, add the chopped meat from 1 or 2 lobster tails to this dish when you cook the shrimp and scallops.

| | | |
|---|---|---|
| 2 Tbsp. | butter | 25 mL |
| 1 Tbsp. | olive oil | 15 mL |
| 12 | large shrimp, peeled, with tail portions left intact | 12 |
| 12 | large sea scallops, each cut in half | 12 |
| 2 | shallots, finely chopped | 2 |
| 2 | garlic cloves, finely chopped | 2 |
| 1 Tbsp. | all-purpose flour | 15 mL |
| 1/2 cup | dry sherry | 125 mL |
| 1 cup | chicken or fish stock | 250 mL |
| 2 Tbsp. | tomato paste | 25 mL |
| 1 tsp. | paprika | 5 mL |
| pinch | cayenne pepper | pinch |
| pinch | dried tarragon | pinch |
| 1/2 cup | whipping cream | 125 mL |
| to taste | salt and white pepper | to taste |
| 2 Tbsp. | chopped fresh parsley | 25 mL |

Heat the butter and oil in a wide skillet over medium-high heat. Add the shrimp and scallops and sauté until just cooked through, about 2–3 minutes. Scoop them onto a plate and set aside.

Add the shallot and garlic to the skillet and cook for 2–3 minutes. Stir in the flour until well combined. Whisk in the sherry and cook, stirring constantly, until a thick sauce forms. Whisk in the stock, tomato paste, paprika, cayenne pepper, tarragon, whipping cream, salt and white pepper. Simmer until the sauce is slightly thickened. Mix in the reserved shrimp and scallops and heat through. Adjust the seasoning, sprinkle with parsley and serve.

# Flounder Parmesan with Herb Tomato Sauce

preparation time · 20 minutes
cooking time · 20 minutes
makes · 4 servings

Here's a seafood version of the classic Italian dish that is usually made with chicken or veal.

| THE SAUCE | | | |
|---|---|---|---|
| | 1 | 14-oz. (398-mL) can tomato sauce | 1 |
| | 1/4 cup | cold water | 50 mL |
| | 1 | garlic clove, crushed | 1 |
| | to taste | salt and freshly cracked black pepper | to taste |
| | 1/2 tsp. | dried oregano | 2 mL |
| | 1/2 tsp. | dried basil | 2 mL |
| | pinch | sugar | pinch |
| **THE FISH** | 1 cup | bread crumbs | 250 mL |
| | 1/2 cup | freshly grated Parmesan cheese | 125 mL |
| | to taste | salt and freshly cracked black pepper | to taste |
| | 1/2 tsp. | dried oregano | 2 mL |
| | 1/2 tsp. | dried basil | 2 mL |
| | 1/2 cup | all-purpose flour | 125 mL |
| | 2 | large eggs beaten with 1/4 cup (50 mL) milk | 2 |
| | 1 1/2 lbs. | flounder fillets, cut, if needed, into 4 portions | 750 g |
| | 3–4 Tbsp. | vegetable oil | 45–60 mL |
| | to garnish | lemon wedges | to garnish |

### THE SAUCE

Combine all the ingredients in a pot over medium heat. Bring to a simmer, cover and cook for 15–20 minutes. Keep warm over low heat until the fish is cooked.

### THE FISH

Combine the bread crumbs, Parmesan cheese, salt, pepper, oregano and basil in a wide shallow bowl. Place the flour in another bowl and the egg mixture in a third bowl.

Coat the flounder in flour, shaking off any excess. Dip the fish in the egg mixture, ensuring it is evenly coated. Set the fillets in the bread crumb mixture and coat on both sides, gently pressing the crumbs on.

Heat the oil in a large non-stick skillet over medium-high heat. Cook the flounder for 3–4 minutes per side, until nicely coloured and cooked through.

Spoon the sauce onto serving plates and set the fish on top. Garnish with lemon wedges and serve.

### ERIC'S OPTIONS

For convenience, the herb tomato sauce can be replaced with a jar of your favourite store-bought tomato-based pasta sauce. Substitute other fish fillets, such as sole, cod or snapper, for the flounder.

# Curried Steamed Fish with Asian-Style Vegetables

preparation time · 20 minutes
cooking time · 10 minutes
makes · 2 servings

Serve this light and healthy fish with steamed long-grain, jasmine or basmati rice and dinner is ready.

| ERIC'S OPTIONS | | | |
|---|---|---|---|
| If you can't find fresh shiitake mushrooms, replace with an equal amount of medium white or brown mushrooms cut in half. | 2 | 5- to 6-oz. (150- to 175-g) fish fillets, such as monkfish, skate, halibut or salmon | 2 |
| | 1 Tbsp. | mild, medium or hot curry paste | 15 mL |
| | 2–3 | baby bok choy, trimmed and separated into leaves | 2–3 |
| | 10 | snow or snap peas, trimmed | 10 |
| | 8 | baby corn | 8 |
| | 1 | small red pepper, halved and cubed | 1 |
| | 1 | small carrot, cut in thin diagonal slices | 1 |
| | 6–8 | fresh shiitake mushrooms, steams removed | 6–8 |
| | 1 Tbsp. | sesame seeds, toasted (see Note on page 128) | 15 mL |
| | 2 Tbsp. | chopped cilantro or green onion | 25 mL |

Rub or brush the fish fillets with curry paste. Cover and marinate in the fridge, if time allows, for 1 hour. Line a bamboo steamer with bok choy leaves (the steamer I use is 11 inches/28 cm in diameter). Set the fish in the steamer. Artfully arrange the peas, corn, red pepper, carrot and mushrooms around the fish. Place the lid on the steamer and set in a wok, skillet or pot filled with boiling water to a level just below the steamer. Steam for 10 minutes, or until the fish and vegetables are just cooked through. Serve from the steamer, garnished with the cilantro or onion.

# Clams Steamed with Pancetta, Tomatoes and Wine

preparation time · 15 minutes
cooking time · 10 minutes
makes · 2–3 servings

Pancetta is Italian-style bacon that is cured with salt and spices, but not smoked. One of its uses in Italian cooking is to flavour sauces, such as this colourful fresh tomato and herb-flecked one. You can buy pancetta at Italian food stores and some supermarkets.

**ERIC'S OPTIONS**
For a Spanish-style sauce, use 1 grilled, cooled and finely chopped chorizo sausage instead of the pancetta. Add it to the pot with the tomatoes. Increase the olive oil to 2 Tbsp (25 mL) to replace the fat from the pancetta.

| | | |
|---|---|---|
| 1 Tbsp. | olive oil | 15 mL |
| 1/4 lb. | pancetta, finely chopped | 125 g |
| 1/2 | medium onion, finely chopped | 1/2 |
| 3 | garlic cloves, chopped | 3 |
| 1/2 cup | dry white wine | 125 mL |
| 3 | ripe, medium tomatoes, halved, seeds removed and chopped | 3 |
| 2–3 Tbsp. | chopped fresh basil or oregano | 25–45 mL |
| pinch | sugar | pinch |
| to taste | freshly cracked black pepper | to taste |
| 2 lbs. | fresh clams, rinsed in cold water | 1 kg |

Heat the oil in a pot over medium-high heat. Add the pancetta and cook until crispy. Drain off all but 2 Tbsp. (25 mL) of the oil and rendered fat from the pan. Add the onion and garlic and cook until tender, about 3–4 minutes. Add the wine, tomatoes, basil or oregano, sugar and pepper. Simmer for 5 minutes. Add the clams, cover the pot and cook until the clams just open. Divide the clams and sauce among bowls and serve.

# Poached Sablefish
# with Champagne Hollandaise

preparation time · 40 minutes
cooking time · 20 minutes
makes · 4 servings

Sablefish is a sleek, black-skinned fish harvested from the cold, deep waters of the North Pacific. For years it was most often smoked and was known as black cod, and still is in some areas. Restaurant chefs and knowledgeable home cooks now prefer it unsmoked. With its pearly white flesh and sweet, rich flavour, it's easy to understand why.

| | | | |
|---|---|---|---|
| **THE HOLLANDAISE** | 3 | large egg yolks | 3 |
| | 1/4 cup | Champagne or sparkling wine | 50 mL |
| | 1/4 lb. | butter, melted | 125 g |
| | 2 Tbsp. | finely chopped green onions or chives | 25 mL |
| | to taste | salt and white pepper | to taste |
| **THE FISH** | 1 cup | dry white wine | 250 mL |
| | 3 cups | fish stock or water | 750 mL |
| | 2 | bay leaves | 2 |
| | 1 | medium onion, thinly sliced | 1 |
| | 2 | garlic cloves, thinly sliced | 2 |
| | 3–4 | lemon slices | 3–4 |
| | 1/2 tsp. | dried thyme | 2 mL |
| | 1/2 tsp. | whole black peppercorns | 2 mL |
| | 4 | parsley sprigs | 4 |
| | 4 | 5-oz. (150-g) sablefish fillets | 4 |

### THE HOLLANDAISE

Place the egg yolks in a heatproof bowl and whisk in the wine. Place the bowl over (but not touching) boiling water and whisk steadily until the mixture begins to lighten and thicken like lightly whipped cream. Remove from the heat and very, very slowly whisk in the melted butter. Mix in the onion or chives and season with salt and pepper. Cover the bowl with plastic wrap and keep the sauce warm (not hot, or the eggs will cook), until the fish is cooked.

### THE FISH

Place the wine, stock or water, bay leaves, onion, garlic and lemon in a medium-sized pot. Tie the thyme, peppercorns and parsley in a piece of cheesecloth. Drop into the wine mixture. Bring the mixture to a simmer over medium heat and simmer for 10 minutes. Add the fish fillets. Cover and simmer for 7–8 minutes, or until the fish is just cooked through.

Remove the fish to serving plates, using a large slotted spoon or lifter. Top each fillet with a spoonful of the hollandaise, and serve the rest alongside.

**ERIC'S OPTIONS**
To make the poaching liquid a little more upscale and give the fish a golden hue, add 1/2 tsp. (2 mL) of crumbled saffron threads when you add the wine. The poaching liquid can be used to cook just about any kind of fish fillets or steaks, such as salmon, cod, halibut and skate. For a less fussy alternative to hollandaise sauce, try White Wine Chive Sauce, page 174.

# Boiled Lobster or Dungeness Crab

preparation time · 5 minutes
cooking time · 9–10 minutes
makes · 2 servings

You never want to overcook lobster or crab or your investment will turn to rubber. Once the lobster or crab is in the pot and the water returns to a boil, I allow 4 minutes for the first pound (500 g) and about 3 minutes for each additional pound (500 g). If the lobster or crab has a softer shell, I shorten this cooking a tiny bit more.

| | | |
|---|---|---|
| 1/4 cup | sea salt | 50 mL |
| 2 | 1 1/2-lb. (750-g) live lobsters or Dungeness crabs | 2 |
| | lemon wedges | |

Bring 1 1/2 gallons (6 litres) of water to a rapid boil in a large pot. Add the salt and return to a boil. Add the lobsters or crabs, return to a boil, and cook for 5–6 minutes, or until just cooked through. Carefully remove them from the pot, holding them above the water to allow them to drain, and place on dinner plates. Serve with lemon wedges and, if desired, bowls of warm melted butter.

## ERIC'S OPTIONS

For each additional lobster or crab you wish to cook, use an additional 2 cups (500 mL) water and 2 Tbsp. (25 mL) salt. To make it easier to place the live lobster or crab in the pot, place on a tray in the freezer, or submerged in crushed ice, for 15 minutes or so before cooking. This more or less puts it to sleep, making it easier to slip it into the pot. Add an extra minute to the cooking time, as the lobster or crab will be quite cold. Instead of boiling the lobster or crab, it can be steamed. Place in a large, wide stainless steel or bamboo steamer set over boiling water. Cover and cook for 5–6 minutes, until just cooked through.

Some cooks prefer to clean their crab before boiling; noting that cooking them with their innards negatively affects flavour. If you go this route (see How to Clean a Live Crab, page 121), cooking time, once the crab is added and the water returns to a boil, will be 3–4 minutes.

### HOW TO CLEAN A LIVE CRAB

Cleaning a live crab before boiling or steaming makes it easier to eat once cooked.

The raw, cleaned crab halves can be grilled, broiled or baked, or cut into smaller pieces and used in stir-fries, paella, soups and stews.

Place the crab on a tray in the freezer or submerge it in crushed ice for 15 minutes or so. This more or less puts it to sleep, making it easier to clean.

Place the crab on its back. Place a large, heavy knife firmly along the centre-line of the crab, between the two sets of legs. Firmly strike the knife with a rubber mallet or similar tool, cutting it in half. This kills the crab, but it will continue to move for a few minutes.

When it has stopped moving, remove the triangular-shaped apron from the underside of the crab. Pull off the top shell. Remove and discard the gills (feathery fingers situated beside the legs) and the beaklike mouth parts. Pull and rinse away the other innards. The two cleaned halves of crab are now ready to be used.

### HOW TO CLEAN A COOKED CRAB

Cooked whole crabs are available at many stores selling seafood. If the retailer does not provide a service to clean and prepare it for cooking or eating, you can do it yourself. Turn the crab over and twist off the triangular-shaped tail apron near the back legs. Turn the crab upright. Hold the legs down with one hand, and use the other hand to pull off the top shell. Pull away and discard the gills from each side of the crab. Rinse out the inner cavity. Break off the legs where they join the body. Cut the body into halves or quarters. If desired, carefully crack the legs and claws with a kitchen mallet or back of a knife. Or provide crab crackers and diners can to crack it open themselves at the table.

# BRILLIANTLYBAKED

CHAPTER SEVEN

# Salmon and Shrimp Bake with Mandarin Ginger Glaze

preparation time · 25 minutes
cooking time · about 20 minutes
makes · 4 servings

Serve this Asian-style seafood dish with steamed rice and a simple stir-fry of green beans, red bell peppers and water chestnuts.

**ERIC'S OPTIONS**
Small, regular orange slices and juice can be used when mandarin oranges are unavailable. For a sweet, sour and spicy taste, mix Asian-style chili sauce to taste into the mandarin orange juice mixture before spooning over the salmon.

| | | |
|---|---|---|
| 2 Tbsp. | butter, softened | 25 mL |
| 4 | 5-oz. (150-g) salmon fillets | 4 |
| 2–3 | mandarin oranges, peeled and thinly sliced into rounds | 2–3 |
| 8 | large shrimp, peeled, with tail portion left intact | 8 |
| to taste | salt and freshly cracked black pepper | to taste |
| 1 cup | mandarin orange juice | 250 mL |
| 2 Tbsp. | lemon juice | 25 mL |
| 1 tsp. | grated fresh ginger | 5 mL |
| 1 | garlic clove, crushed | 1 |
| pinch | cayenne pepper | pinch |
| 1 tsp. | cornstarch | 5 mL |
| 1 Tbsp. | brown sugar | 15 mL |
| 2 | green onions, finely chopped | 2 |

Preheat the oven to 425°F (220°C). Brush a shallow baking dish with the butter. Set the salmon fillets in the dish, leaving enough space between them so they can easily be lifted out. Top each salmon fillet with 2–3 mandarin slices and 2 shrimp. Season with salt and pepper.

Place the orange juice, lemon juice, ginger, garlic, cayenne, cornstarch and brown sugar in a small pot and whisk to combine. Boil until very slightly thickened. Evenly spoon the glaze over each salmon portion. Bake for 15–20 minutes, or until the salmon and shrimp are just cooked through. Lift the fillets out carefully and set on plates. Spoon the juices from the baking dish over top. Sprinkle with the green onions and serve.

## WHEN IS SEAFOOD COOKED?

When touched, cooked fish should feel slightly firm, not hard—a sign you have overcooked it—and not soft—a sign it's not cooked through. When cooked, the flesh will also start to slightly separate into flakes, and it will lose its translucency and become opaque. With some fish, such as salmon, a white deposit of fat seeps out between the flakes when cooked. The old fisherman's rule of thumb for cooking time is to allow 10 minutes per inch (2.5 cm) of thickness, no matter if the fish is whole or cut into fillets or steaks. I've tried it and it seems to work, when moderate cooking temperatures are used. Shellfish, such as shrimp or scallops, cook quickly. Like fish, the flesh should feel slightly firm when cooked, but not hard. Clams and mussel are done when their shells open. The longer you cook them after they open, the tougher they become.

# Lemon Thyme-Roasted Salmon on White Kidney Bean Stew

preparation time · 20 minutes
cooking time · 37–45 minutes
makes · 4 servings

Here's a tasty dish with a healthy excuse to eat it. Salmon is high in protein and is also a rich source of vitamin A, the B-group vitamins and Omega-3 oils. White kidney beans are also rich in protein and a good source of iron, phosphorus and calcium.

ERIC'S OPTIONS
Other canned legumes, such as chickpeas, black-eyed peas or pinto beans, can be substituted for white kidney beans. For added richness, drizzle the salmon tableside with a little extra virgin olive oil.

| | | |
|---|---|---|
| 2 Tbsp. | olive oil | 25 mL |
| 1 | medium onion, finely chopped | 1 |
| 1 | medium carrot, finely chopped | 1 |
| 2 | garlic cloves, finely chopped | 2 |
| 1 | 19-oz. (540-mL) can white kidney beans, drained well | 1 |
| 1 | 14-oz. (398-mL) can diced tomatoes | 1 |
| 1/2 cup | fish, chicken or vegetable stock | 125 mL |
| pinch | sugar | pinch |
| 1 Tbsp. | fresh thyme leaves, minced | 15 mL |
| 4 | 5-oz. (150-g) salmon fillets | 4 |
| 1 | lemon, juice of | 1 |
| to taste | salt and freshly cracked black pepper | to taste |
| to garnish | thyme sprigs | to garnish |

Heat the olive oil in a pot over medium heat. Add the onion, carrot and garlic and cook until tender, about 5 minutes. Add the kidney beans, tomatoes, stock, sugar and 1 tsp. (5 mL) of the thyme. Simmer for 20–25 minutes.

Preheat the oven to 375°F (190°C). Place the salmon on a non-stick or parchment-lined baking sheet. Sprinkle with the lemon juice, salt, pepper and the remaining 2 tsp. (10 mL) of minced thyme. Bake for 12–15 minutes, or until cooked through.

Season the kidney bean mixture with salt and pepper, then spoon it into shallow serving bowls. Top with a piece of salmon, garnish with thyme sprigs and serve.

# Nori-Wrapped Salmon with Maple-Wasabi Teriyaki Sauce

preparation time · 15 minutes
cooking time · 12–15 minutes
makes · 4 servings

If you've made sushi and don't know what to do with the leftover nori sheets, this Japanese-inspired dish offers another way of using them.

**ERIC'S OPTIONS**
Instead of baking the salmon, try steaming in a large bamboo steamer. It gives the salmon a softer, moister exterior. Line a large bamboo steamer with a perforated piece of parchment paper or nori. Set the salmon inside. Set the steamer in a wok or large skillet filled with boiling water to a level just below the steamer. Cover and steam until just cooked through, about 10 minutes.

| | | |
|---|---|---|
| 3/4 cup | teriyaki sauce | 175 mL |
| 1/4 cup | maple syrup | 50 mL |
| 1 | garlic clove, crushed | 1 |
| 1 tsp. | grated fresh ginger | 5 mL |
| 2 Tbsp. | rice wine vinegar | 25 mL |
| 2 | green onions, finely chopped | 2 |
| 1 tsp. | wasabi powder, or to taste | 5 mL |
| 4 | 5-oz. (150-g) salmon fillets | 4 |
| 1 | nori sheet, cut into 4 strips | 1 |

Preheat the oven to 425°F (220°C). Make the sauce by combining 1/4 cup (50 mL) of the teriyaki sauce with the maple syrup, garlic, ginger, vinegar, green onions and wasabi powder in a bowl. Cover and refrigerate until the salmon is cooked.

Place the salmon in a dish with sides. Pour in the remaining teriyaki sauce and marinate in the fridge for 1 hour, turning occasionally.

Place the nori strips on a work surface. Remove the salmon from the marinade and set a piece of salmon at the end of each strip of nori. Roll the nori around the salmon and place on a parchment-lined baking sheet. Brush the top of the salmon with the marinade. Bake for 12–15 minutes, or until the salmon is cooked through. Serve with small bowls of the sauce alongside for dipping.

# Miso-Glazed Salmon Steaks

| | | |
|---|---|---|
| preparation time | · | 10 minutes |
| cooking time | · | 12–15 minutes |
| makes | · | 4 servings |

Miso, fermented soybean paste, is widely used in Japanese cooking and is sold in Japanese food stores and some supermarkets and health food stores. Its intense salty flavour anchors this delicious glaze for salmon steaks.

**NOTE**
To toast sesame seeds, place in a non-stick skillet over medium heat. Cook, swirling the pan from time to time, for 5 minutes, or until lightly toasted.

| | | |
|---|---|---|
| 3 Tbsp. | melted butter | 45 mL |
| 4 | 6-oz. (170-g) salmon steaks | 4 |
| 3 Tbsp. | white (shiro) miso paste | 45 mL |
| 1 Tbsp. | soy sauce | 15 mL |
| 1 Tbsp. | rice vinegar | 15 mL |
| 1 Tbsp. | brown sugar | 15 mL |
| to taste | Asian-style hot chili sauce | to taste |
| 2 | green onions, finely chopped | 2 |
| 1 Tbsp. | sesame seeds, toasted (see Note) | 15 mL |

Preheat the oven to 425°F (220°C). Brush the bottom of a shallow baking dish with 1 Tbsp. (15 mL) of the melted butter. Place the salmon steaks in the dish. Whisk the remaining melted butter with the miso, soy sauce, vinegar, brown sugar and chili sauce in a bowl. Spoon the mixture over the salmon. Bake for 12–15 minutes, or until the salmon is just cooked through. Place on serving plates and spoon the pan juices over top. Sprinkle with chopped green onions and toasted sesame seeds.

### ERIC'S OPTIONS
For a smoky taste, cook the salmon on the barbecue. Preheat the grill to medium. Cut 2 sheets of foil, each 2 feet (60 cm) long, and place one on top of the other. Brush the centre with 1 Tbsp. (15 mL) melted butter. Place the salmon steaks on top. Make the miso glaze, then pour over the salmon. Fold up the sides of the foil and pinch to seal. Barbecue for 15–20 minutes, or until cooked through.

Cornmeal-Crusted
Oyster Burgers   page 84

Thai-Style
Fish Cakes    page 90

Lemon Pepper
Snapper   page 100

Deviled Skate with Lemon
Parsley Mayonnaise   page 104

Curried Steamed Fish with
Asian-Style Vegetables    page 116

Pan-Seared Scallops on
Ginger-Spiked Mango Sauce    page 108

Clams Steamed with Pancetta, Tomatoes and Wine  page 117

Salmon and Shrimp Bake with
Mandarin Ginger Glaze   page 124

# Haddock and Winter Vegetable Casserole

preparation time · 25 minutes
cooking time · 20 minutes
makes · 4 servings

Here's a complete meal that is inexpensive to make and can be baked in one pan. Try it for a winter Sunday dinner.

**ERIC'S OPTIONS**
Use cod, snapper, salmon or halibut fillets if haddock is unavailable. If you wish, replace the wine with stock.

| | | |
|---|---|---|
| 3 Tbsp. | melted butter | 45 mL |
| 4 | medium red-skinned potatoes, cut into wedges | 4 |
| 2 | medium carrots, halved lengthwise and sliced diagonally | 2 |
| 2 cups | chopped green cabbage | 500 mL |
| 4 | 5-oz. (150-g) haddock fillets | 4 |
| to taste | salt and freshly cracked black pepper | to taste |
| 1/2 cup | white wine | 125 mL |
| 1/2 cup | fish, chicken or vegetable stock | 125 mL |
| 2 | garlic cloves, finely chopped | 2 |
| 1/2 cup | frozen peas | 125 mL |
| 1 Tbsp. | chopped fresh parsley | 15 mL |

Preheat the oven to 425°F (220°C). Brush a 9- x 13-inch (3.5 L) baking dish with 1 Tbsp. (15 mL) of the melted butter. Place the potatoes and carrots in a large pot and cover with 3 inches (8 cm) of cold water. Bring to a boil and cook until firm-tender. Add the cabbage and cook just until it brightens in colour, about 2 minutes. Drain the vegetables well and place in the casserole. Set the haddock fillets on top; season with salt and pepper. Combine the remaining butter, wine, stock and garlic in a bowl. Spoon the mixture over the haddock and vegetables. Sprinkle in the frozen peas. Cover and bake for 20 minutes, or until the haddock is cooked through. Sprinkle with the parsley and serve.

# Greek-Style Snapper Fillets

preparation time · 10 minutes
cooking time · 15–20 minutes
makes · 4 servings

Serve this quick, Greek-style fish dish with boiled potatoes and a mix of steamed green beans and wax beans.

**ERIC'S OPTIONS**
Use other fish fillets, such as halibut, haddock or cod, instead of snapper. For added colour, use a mix of green and black olives.

| | | | |
|---|---|---|---|
| 4 | 5- to 6-oz. (150- to 175-g) snapper fillets | 4 |
| to taste | salt and freshly cracked black pepper | to taste |
| 1/3 cup | fish, chicken or vegetable stock | 75 mL |
| 1/3 cup | black olives, whole | 75 mL |
| 1/2 cup | coarsely crumbled feta cheese | 125 mL |
| 8–12 | cherry tomatoes, halved | 8–12 |
| 2 Tbsp. | extra virgin olive oil | 25 mL |
| 1/2 | lemon, juice of | 1/2 |
| 2 Tbsp. | chopped fresh oregano | 25 mL |

Preheat the oven to 425°F (220°C). Arrange the snapper fillets in a single layer in a shallow baking dish; season with salt and pepper. Pour in the stock. Top the fish with the olives, feta and cherry tomatoes. Drizzle with the olive oil and lemon juice; sprinkle with oregano. Bake for 15 minutes, or until the fish is cooked through. Divide the fish and other ingredients between 4 heated plates.

# Oven-Baked
# Fish and Chips

preparation time · 10 minutes
cooking time · 30–35 minutes
makes · 4 servings

No deep-fryer, no problem. Use this recipe the next time you have a craving for fish and chips. Serve with lemon slices, Tartar Sauce (page 171) and Creamy Coleslaw (page 164).

**ERIC'S OPTIONS**
If you are watching your salt intake, consider replacing the seasoning salt with a mix of your own seasonings, such as freshly ground pepper, lemon pepper, paprika, garlic granules and dried herbs.

| | | |
|---|---|---|
| 3 | medium baking potatoes | 3 |
| 3 Tbsp. | vegetable oil | 45 mL |
| to taste | seasoning salt | to taste |
| 4 | 5- to 6-oz. (150- to 175-g) fish fillets, such as cod, haddock, halibut or salmon | 4 |

Preheat the oven to 425°F (220°C). Cut the potatoes in half lengthwise. Cut each half into 4–6 wedges. Place the wedges in a bowl and toss with the oil and seasoning salt. Arrange the potatoes in a single layer on a large non-stick or parchment-lined baking sheet. Bake for 15 minutes, turn the potatoes over and bake for 5 minutes more. Sprinkle the fish with seasoning salt. Make a spot for each piece of fish among the potatoes. Continue baking until the fish is cooked through, about 10–15 minutes more.

# Ricotta-Stuffed Squid
# with Olive Tomato Sauce

preparation time · 40 minutes
cooking time · 70 minutes
makes · 4–6 servings

The long, slow braising makes the squid mouth-wateringly tender. Serve with your favourite bite-sized pasta and a mixed green salad.

**NOTE**

To toast pine nuts, bake in a 350°F (180°C) oven for 12–15 minutes, or until lightly toasted.

| | | |
|---|---|---|
| 1 | 1/2-lb. (250-g) tub ricotta cheese | 1 |
| 1 | 10-oz. (300-g) package frozen chopped spinach, thawed and moisture squeezed out | 1 |
| 2 Tbsp. | freshly grated Parmesan cheese | 25 mL |
| to taste | salt and freshly ground black pepper | to taste |
| pinch | nutmeg | pinch |
| 2 Tbsp. | chopped fresh basil or parsley, plus some to sprinkle on top | 25 mL |
| 1 | egg, slightly beaten | 1 |
| 12 | 5- to 6-inch long (12- to 15-cm), squid tubes, patted dry | 12 |
| 3 Tbsp. | olive oil | 45 mL |
| 1 | medium onion, finely chopped | 1 |
| 2 | garlic cloves, finely chopped | 2 |
| 1 | 14-oz. (398-mL) can tomato sauce | 1 |
| 1/2 cup | white wine | 125 mL |
| 1/3 cup | chopped black olives | 75 mL |
| pinch | sugar | pinch |
| 3–4 Tbsp. | pine nuts, lightly toasted | 45–60 mL |

Place the ricotta cheese, spinach, Parmesan cheese, salt, pepper, nutmeg, basil or parsley and egg in a bowl. Mix well to combine. Stuff the mixture into the squid tubes, filling them about half full. (To more easily stuff squid, spoon the filling into a piping bag fitted with a plain tip and pipe the mixture into the squid tubes. Otherwise, use a small spoon.) Secure the opening of each squid tube with a toothpick.

Preheat the oven to 350°F (180°C). Heat the oil over medium-high heat in a large skillet. Lightly brown the squid on both sides. Place in a single layer in a large, shallow casserole. Add the onion and garlic to the skillet and cook until tender, about 5 minutes. Add the tomato sauce, wine, olives and sugar to the skillet. Bring to a simmer and then pour the sauce around the squid. Cover and bake for 1 hour. Remove the toothpicks from the squid and divide among heated plates. Spoon the sauce around the squid, sprinkle with the pine nuts and a little chopped basil or parsley and serve.

ERIC'S OPTIONS
For added colour in the sauce, use a mix of black and green olives. To make it spicier, sprinkle crushed chili flakes to taste into the sauce before baking.

# Almost Lobster Thermidor for Two

preparation time · 40 minutes
cooking time · about 20 minutes
makes · 2 servings

I call this "almost" lobster thermidor because, unlike tradional recipes for the dish, which call for egg yolks and buckets of cream, this lighter version uses no egg yolk and only 1/2 cup (125 mL) of whipping cream. Serve this refined dish on special occasions, such as Valentine's Day or Monday night. Serve with steamed asparagus and Saffron Rice (page 168).

**ERIC'S OPTIONS**

No sherry? Use brandy in the sauce instead. This dish can be made oven-ready several hours in advance. Cover and store in the fridge until you're ready to bake it. Allow a few more minutes baking time as you will be starting from cold.

| | | |
|---|---|---|
| 1 | 1 1/2-lb. (750-g) live lobster | 1 |
| 1 Tbsp. | butter | 15 mL |
| 1/3 lb. | mushrooms, thinly sliced | 170 g |
| 1 | garlic clove, finely chopped | 1 |
| 1/4 tsp. | paprika | 1 mL |
| 1/4 tsp. | dried tarragon | 1 mL |
| 1 oz. | dry sherry | 30 mL |
| 1/2 cup | whipping cream | 125 mL |
| to taste | salt and white pepper | to taste |
| 2–3 Tbsp. | freshly grated Parmesan cheese | 25–45 mL |

Bring 1 gallon (4 L) of water to a boil. Add 2 Tbsp. (25 mL) of salt to the pot. Add the lobster, return to a boil and cook for 3 minutes, or until slightly underdone. Remove from the pot, drain well and place on a tray. When the lobster is cool enough to handle, twist off the claws, crack them and carefully remove the meat. Cut the lobster body in half lengthwise, beginning from the tail end. Remove the tail meat. Cut all the lobster meat into 1/4-inch (5-mm) pieces, and place on a plate. Rinse out the cavity of the lobster and pat dry. Place cut-side up in a baking dish and set aside.

Preheat the oven to 425°F (220°C). Melt the butter in a skillet over medium heat. Add the mushrooms and cook until they're tender and the liquid has evaporated. Add the garlic, paprika and tarragon and cook for 1 minute more. Add the sherry and cook until it has almost evaporated. Add the whipping cream and reduce until the mixture thickens lightly. Stir in the reserved lobster meat and remove from the heat. Season with salt and pepper.

Mound the lobster mixture into the lobster shells. Sprinkle with Parmesan cheese. Bake for 10–12 minutes, until golden and just heated through.

# Citrus-Baked Monkfish

preparation time · 20 minutes
cooking time · 12–15 minutes
makes · 4 servings

Citrus and olives give this monkfish a taste of the Mediterranean. Monkfish is sometimes called mock lobster because it has a similar rich, sweetish flavour and firm texture.

ERIC'S OPTIONS
For an additional hit of colour and flavour, add 8–12 halved cherry tomatoes, to the dish just before baking. For added richness, drizzle the monkfish table-side with a little more extra virgin olive oil.

| | | |
|---|---|---|
| 4 | 6-oz. (175-g) monkfish fillets | 4 |
| 1/4 cup | orange juice | 50 mL |
| 2 Tbsp. | extra virgin olive oil | 25 mL |
| 1 Tbsp. | lemon juice | 15 mL |
| 1/4 cup | black olives | 50 mL |
| 1/4 cup | green olives | 50 mL |
| to taste | salt and freshly cracked black pepper | to taste |
| 4 | thin orange slices, peeled | 4 |
| 4 | thin lemon slices, peeled | 4 |
| 2 Tbsp. | chopped fresh oregano or basil | 25 mL |
| to garnish | oregano or basil sprigs | to garnish |

Preheat the oven to 425°F (220°C). Trim any grey outer membrane from the monkfish and place the fish in a shallow baking dish. Drizzle with the orange juice, olive oil and lemon juice. Surround with the olives. Season with salt and pepper. Top each piece of monkfish with 1 orange and 1 lemon slice. Sprinkle with the chopped oregano or basil. Bake for 12–15 minutes, or until cooked through. Place on heated plates and spoon the pan juices over top. Garnish with sprigs of oregano or basil.

# Moroccan-Spiced Grouper Fillets

preparation time · 10 minutes
cooking time · 12–15 minutes
makes · 4 servings

The intense blend of spices does three jobs in this recipe: it gives the fish a beautiful, golden colour, an inviting aroma and a mildly spicy, intriguing taste.

**ERIC'S OPTIONS**
Try other fish fillets, such as halibut or salmon. Serve the fish with Papaya Ginger Salsa (see Grilled Marlin Steaks with Papaya Ginger Salsa, page 146).

| | | |
|---|---|---|
| 4 | 5- to 6-oz. (150- to 175-g) grouper fillets | 4 |
| 2 Tbsp. | olive oil | 25 mL |
| 1/2 tsp. | ground cumin | 2 mL |
| 1/2 tsp. | ground coriander seed | 2 mL |
| 1/2 tsp. | freshly cracked black pepper | 2 mL |
| 1/2 tsp. | salt | 2 mL |
| 1/4 tsp. | cayenne pepper | 1 mL |
| 2 tsp. | freshly grated lemon zest | 10 mL |
| 2 Tbsp. | honey, slightly warmed | 25 mL |

Place the grouper in a single layer in a non-stick or parchment-lined shallow baking dish. Brush with olive oil. Combine the cumin, coriander, pepper, salt, cayenne and lemon zest in a small bowl. Rub this spice mixture on the fish. Cover and marinate in the fridge for 30 minutes, then bring to room temperature.

Preheat the oven to 375°F (190°C). Drizzle the fish with honey. Bake for 12–15 minutes, or until cooked through.

# Sole with Mushroom Dill Sauce

preparation time · 25 minutes
cooking time · 15 minutes
makes · 4 servings

Mild, delicate-tasting sole is richly enhanced by this dill-flecked sauce.

**ERIC'S OPTIONS**
Try other herbs in the sauce, or use a mix, such as tarragon, chives or parsley alone or in combination with the dill. The sauce is good with other baked or pan-fried fish fillets, such as cod, flounder, salmon, halibut, haddock or snapper.

| | | |
|---|---|---|
| 4 large or 8 small | sole fillets | 4 large or 8 small |
| 1/4 cup | melted butter | 50 mL |
| 2 Tbsp. | lemon juice | 25 mL |
| to taste | salt and white pepper | to taste |
| 1/2 | medium onion, finely chopped | 1/2 |
| 1/2 lb. | white or brown mushrooms, thinly sliced | 250 g |
| 2 Tbsp. | all-purpose flour | 25 mL |
| 1 1/2 cups | fish, chicken or vegetable stock | 375 mL |
| 2 tsp. | chopped fresh dill | 10 mL |
| 3 Tbsp. | whipping cream | 45 mL |
| to garnish | dill sprigs | to garnish |

Preheat the oven to 425°F (220°C). Roll the sole fillets into loose cylinders and place in a shallow baking dish. Drizzle with 2 Tbsp. (25 mL) of the melted butter and the lemon juice. Season with salt and white pepper.

Heat the remaining 2 Tbsp. (25 mL) butter in a pot over medium heat. Add the onion and mushrooms and cook until tender, about 5 minutes. Stir in the flour, mixing until well combined. Slowly whisk in the stock, and bring to a simmer. Remove from the heat and set aside.

Bake the sole for 15 minutes, or until just cooked through. Meanwhile, finish the sauce by stirring in the dill and whipping cream. Season with salt and pepper. Return to a simmer and cook until the sauce thickens lightly. Divide the sole among 4 plates. Top with the sauce, garnish with a dill sprig and serve.

# Italian-Style Sole
# Baked in Paper

| | |
|---|---|
| preparation time · | 20 minutes |
| cooking time · | 12–15 minutes |
| makes · | 2 servings |

Cooking fish in parchment paper yields incredible, moist and delicious results even when the fish is slightly overcooked.

**ERIC'S OPTIONS**
Try other fish, such as salmon, flounder or haddock, instead of sole. For a more intense tomato taste, use 2 Tbsp. (25 mL) chopped sun-dried tomatoes. in place of fresh tomatoes. For added colour and flavour, add a few black or green olives before sealing the fish in the parchment.

| | | |
|---|---|---|
| 2 | 5- to 6-oz. (150- to 175-g) sole fillets | 2 |
| 4 | artichoke hearts, quartered | 4 |
| 1 | medium tomato, halved, seeds removed and chopped | 1 |
| 1 Tbsp. | extra virgin olive oil | 15 mL |
| 1/2 | lemon, juice of | 1/2 |
| 2 Tbsp. | dry white wine | 25 mL |
| 1 | garlic clove, finely chopped | 1 |
| 2 Tbsp. | chopped fresh basil | 25 mL |
| to taste | salt and fresh cracked black pepper | to taste |
| pinch | sugar | pinch |

Preheat the oven to 425°F (220°C). Cut 2 pieces of parchment paper, each 18 x 12 inches (45 x 30 cm). Fold the pieces in half and then unfold. Place a piece of sole on the bottom half of each piece. Top each with the artichokes and tomatoes. Place the olive oil, lemon juice, wine, garlic, basil, salt, pepper and sugar in a bowl and mix to combine. Spoon the mixture over the sole. Fold the paper over the fish and crimp the edges well to seal. Bake on baking tray for 10–12 minutes, or until the paper has browned and puffed and the contents are bubbling inside. Transfer the parchment packages to plates, cut them open with scissors tableside and enjoy!

# 10-Minute Scallops

preparation time · 5 minutes
cooking time · 10 minutes
makes · 2 servings

Here's a quick and simply delicious way to cook scallops.

**ERIC'S OPTIONS**
Use smaller, less expensive bay scallops, about 20–24, instead of sea scallops. Cooking time, because of their smaller size, will be 6 to 8 minutes.

| | | |
|---|---|---|
| 1/4 cup | dry white wine | 50 mL |
| 2 Tbsp. | butter | 25 mL |
| squeeze | lemon juice | squeeze |
| 1/4 tsp. | paprika | 1 mL |
| pinch | cayenne pepper | pinch |
| 1 | garlic clove, finely chopped | 1 |
| 10–12 | large sea scallops | 10–12 |
| to taste | salt and freshly cracked pepper | to taste |
| 1 Tbsp. | chopped fresh parsley | 15 mL |

Preheat the oven to 450°F (230°C). Place the wine, butter, lemon juice, paprika, cayenne and garlic in a small pot and simmer over medium heat for 3–4 minutes. Meanwhile, place the scallops in a single layer in a shallow-sided baking dish, or use two small individual baking dishes. Season the scallops with salt and pepper. Spoon the wine/butter mixture over the scallops. Bake for 10 minutes, or until the scallops are just cooked through. Sprinkle with parsley and serve.

# Seafood Sampler

| | | |
|---|---|---|
| preparation time · | 20 minutes | |
| cooking time · | 12–15 minutes | |
| makes · | 2 servings | |

When you need a dish to impress a date or your spouse, try this. It's simple to make, but fancy in appearance and taste.

**ERIC'S OPTIONS**
This dish can be made oven-ready hours in advance to bake when you're ready to serve. You can also use dill or parsley instead of tarragon.

| | | |
|---|---|---|
| 2 | 3- to 4-oz. (75- to 100-g) fish fillets, such as salmon, halibut, cod, haddock or sole | 2 |
| 4 | large sea scallops | 4 |
| 4 | large shrimp, peeled, with tail portion intact | 4 |
| 2 | medium oysters, shucked and left in the half shell | 2 |
| 1/4 cup | dry white wine | 50 mL |
| 2–3 Tbsp. | melted butter | 25–45 mL |
| 1 Tbsp. | chopped fresh tarragon, or 1 tsp. (5 mL) dried | 15 mL |
| 1 | garlic clove, finely chopped | 1 |
| pinch | paprika and cayenne pepper | pinch |
| to taste | salt, freshly cracked pepper and lemon juice | to taste |
| 1 Tbsp. | freshly grated Parmesan cheese | 15 mL |
| to garnish | lemon wedges | to garnish |

Preheat the oven to 450°F (230°C). Place the fish, scallops, shrimp and oysters in a single layer in a shallow baking dish. Combine the wine, butter, tarragon, garlic, paprika, cayenne, salt, pepper and lemon juice in a bowl. Drizzle over the seafood. Sprinkle the Parmesan cheese on the oysters. Bake for 12–15 minutes, or until the seafood is just cooked. Serve straight out of the baking dish, or arrange on plates, spooning the pan juices over top. Garnish with lemon wedges.

# Seafood and Yukon Gold Mashed Potato Casserole

preparation time · 40 minutes
cooking time · 35–40 minutes
makes · 6 servings

This recipe was my teenage son's suggestion. He's fond of shepherd's pie and wondered about making a similar dish with seafood instead of meat. Sounded like a good idea to me!

| THE POTATOES | 2 lbs. | Yukon gold potatoes, peeled and cubed | 1 kg |
|---|---|---|---|
| | 2–3 Tbsp. | butter | 25–45 mL |
| | 1/2–3/4 cup | milk | 125–175 mL |
| | to taste | salt and white pepper | to taste |
| | | | |
| THE FILLING | 3 Tbsp. | butter | 45 mL |
| | 1/2 lb. | firm fish fillets, such as halibut or salmon, cut into cubes | 250 g |
| | 1/4 lb. | small scallops | 125 g |
| | 1 cup | finely chopped onion | 250 mL |
| | 1/2 cup | grated carrot | 125 mL |
| | 1 | garlic clove, finely chopped | 1 |
| | 2 Tbsp. | all-purpose flour | 25 mL |
| | 1 1/4 cups | fish, chicken or vegetable stock | 300 mL |
| | 1/2 tsp. | dried thyme | 2 mL |
| | pinch | cayenne pepper | pinch |
| | 1/2 cup | light cream or milk | 125 mL |
| | 1/2 cup | frozen peas | 125 mL |
| | 1/2 cup | frozen corn | 125 mL |
| | 1/4 lb. | small cooked shrimp | 125 g |
| | to taste | salt and white pepper | to taste |

### THE POTATOES

Boil the potatoes in slightly salted water until tender. Drain well. Mash thoroughly and beat in the remaining ingredients until well combined and the potatoes are lightened. Cover and set aside.

### THE FILLING

Preheat the oven to 375°F (190°C). Melt 2 Tbsp. (25 mL) of the butter in a pot over medium heat. Add the fish and scallops and cook until both just begin to firm up, but do not cook all the way through. Scoop them out and set aside. Add the remaining butter to the pot. Add the onion, carrot and garlic and cook, stirring, until they soften, about 5 minutes. Mix in the flour until well combined. Slowly add the stock, whisking steadily, until incorporated. Add the thyme and cayenne and bring to a simmer. Cook until the mixture begins to thicken. Remove from the heat and mix in the cream or milk, peas, corn, shrimp and reserved fish and scallops. Season with salt and pepper. Spoon the filling into a 9-inch (23-cm) deep-dish pie plate or similar-sized baking dish. Carefully spread the potatoes on top. Bake for 35–40 minutes, until the top is golden and the filling is bubbling.

ERIC'S OPTIONS
If you're only feeding one or two people, divide the filling and potatoes among small baking dishes. Cool surplus portions to room temperature. Tightly wrap them, label and freeze for another meal. Thaw them in the fridge overnight before baking. Baking time for smaller casseroles will be shortened by about 10 minutes.

# Smoked Salmon, Swiss Cheese and Asparagus Quiche

| | | |
|---|---|---|
| preparation time | · | 25 minutes |
| cooking time | · | 40–45 minutes |
| makes | · | 6 servings |

Here's a great dish to serve for a special brunch or lunch. It can be made in advance, cooled and kept in the fridge for one or two days. To reheat, cover loosely and bake in a 300°F (150°C) oven for 25 to 30 minutes.

**ERIC'S OPTIONS**
Make a mixed seafood quiche by replacing 2/3 of the smoked salmon with 1/2 cup (125 mL) of salad shrimp and 1/2 cup (125 mL) of crabmeat. If asparagus is unavailable, replace with 1 1/2 cups (375 mL) of small broccoli florets. Cook as described for the asparagus.

| | | |
|---|---|---|
| 4 | large eggs | 4 |
| 1 1/2 cups | light cream or milk | 375 mL |
| to taste | salt and white pepper | to taste |
| pinch | nutmeg | pinch |
| 1/2 lb. | asparagus, trimmed and cut into bite-sized pieces | 250 g |
| 1 1/4 cups | grated Swiss cheese | 300 mL |
| 1 | 9-inch (23-cm) deep-dish pie shell | 1 |
| 1/4 lb. | cold-smoked salmon, chopped | 125 g |
| 3 | green onions, finely chopped | 3 |

Preheat the oven to 350°F (180°C). Beat the eggs in a bowl, then whisk in the cream or milk, salt, pepper and nutmeg. Cook the asparagus in boiling water until just tender. Immerse in cold water to stop the cooking and set the colour. Drain well and pat dry. Place half the cheese in the pie shell. Top with half the asparagus, smoked salmon and green onions. Pour in the egg mixture. Add the remaining cheese, asparagus, smoked salmon and green onions.

Bake for 40 to 45 minutes, until lightly browned and set. Let rest 10 minutes before cutting into portions.

Haddock and Winter
Vegetable Casserole   page 129

**Almost Lobster
Thermidor for Two** page 134

Grilled Marlin Steaks with
Papaya Ginger Salsa  page 146

Grilled Halibut Fillets with Wax Bean
and Roma Tomato Salad  page 154

Italian-Style Sole
Baked in Paper   page 139

Foil-Barbecued
Clams   page 153

Canadian Beer
Batter   page 179

From top to bottom:

**Sesame Ginger Coleslaw**   page 165
**Spring-Style Potato Salad**   page 167
**Technicolour Coleslaw**   page 166

# GRILLED TO PERFECTION

CHAPTER EIGHT

# Grilled Marlin Steaks
## with Papaya Ginger Salsa

preparation time · 20 minutes
cooking time · 6–8 minutes
makes · 4 servings

Marlin is a firm, meaty fish that's perfect for grilling. The bright-tasting, tropical salsa is a fine accent.

**ERIC'S OPTIONS**
If papaya is not available, make the salsa with a medium-sized mango. A wide range of other grilled fish steaks go well with this salsa, such as tuna, salmon and mahi mahi.

| | | |
|---|---|---|
| 1/2 | fresh, ripe papaya, about 1/2 lb. (250 g) peeled and cut into 1/4-inch (5-mm) cubes | 1/2 |
| 1/4 cup | finely chopped green bell pepper | 50 mL |
| 1 | small, ripe tomato, finely chopped | 1 |
| 2 tsp. | grated fresh ginger | 10 mL |
| 2 tsp. | brown sugar | 10 mL |
| 1 | lime, juice of | 1 |
| 1/4 tsp. | cayenne pepper, or to taste | 1 mL |
| 4 | 5-oz. (150-g) marlin steaks | 4 |
| 1 Tbsp. | vegetable oil | 15 mL |
| to taste | salt and freshly cracked black pepper | to taste |
| to garnish | lime slices and cilantro sprigs | to garnish |

Combine the papaya, bell pepper, tomato, ginger, sugar, lime juice and cayenne pepper in a bowl. Cover and let the flavours meld at room temperature for 30 minutes.

Preheat a non-stick or lightly oiled grill to medium-high. Brush the marlin with the oil; season with salt and pepper. Grill for 3–4 minutes per side, or until just cooked. Top each serving with a spoonful of the salsa and serve the rest alongside. Garnish with lime slices and cilantro sprigs.

## FISH: GRILLING TIPS

Firm-fleshed fish, such as marlin, swordfish, tuna, salmon or shark, are best for cooking directly on the grill. To prevent sticking, lightly oil the surface first, unless it's a high-quality non-stick grill. A wire grill basket is good for cooking whole fish, such as snapper or salmon. It is easier to turn the fish and the skin doesn't stick to the grill. Grill baskets also work well for fillets of more fine-textured, fish such as snapper, cod or flounder. Whole fish and tender fish fillets and steaks can also be wrapped in foil with flavourings before cooking on the grill.

Skewer small shellfish, such as shrimp or scallops, or cubes of fish, on metal or water-soaked wooden skewers before cooking so they don't fall through the grill.

Do not use too high a heat when grilling seafood—medium to medium-high is best. (The exception is tuna, which is seared quickly to medium-rare.) Seafood generally cooks quickly. This more moderate cooking temperature allows you to monitor how it's doing. Turn the fish only once. Flipping it back and forth can cause it to break apart.

Seafood flavoured with a dry mix of herbs or spices is less likely to stick to the grill than seafood flavoured with a wet marinade. You can still grill the latter but just be sure to oil the grill generously first or it may fuse to the grill as the marinade heats up.

# Grilled Tuna on Chickpea Salad

| preparation time | · | 20 minutes |
| cooking time | · | 4–6 minutes |
| makes | · | 6 servings |

Fire up the barbecue and serve this dish on a hot summer day. Make the salad in the morning and you'll have dinner in just a few minutes.

| THE SALAD | | | |
|---|---|---|---|
| 1 | lemon, juice of | 1 |
| 3 Tbsp. | olive oil | 45 mL |
| 2 | garlic cloves, crushed | 2 |
| 1/4 cup | chopped fresh basil | 50 mL |
| 1 | 19-oz. (540-mL) can chickpeas, drained, rinsed and drained well again | 1 |
| 1/4 cup | small whole black olives | 50 mL |
| 1/4 cup | small whole green olives | 50 mL |
| 1 | roasted red pepper, halved and sliced | 1 |
| 1/2 | medium onion, finely chopped | 1/2 |
| 2 | medium oranges, peeled, quartered and sliced | 2 |
| to taste | salt and freshly cracked black pepper | to taste |

| THE FISH | | | |
|---|---|---|---|
| 4 | 5-oz. (150-g) tuna steaks | 4 |
| 2 Tbsp. | olive oil | 25 mL |
| to taste | salt and freshly cracked black pepper | to taste |
| to garnish | lemon wedges and Italian parsley sprigs | to garnish |

### THE SALAD

Place all the ingredients in a bowl and mix gently to combine. Cover and let the salad marinate in the fridge for at least an hour.

### THE FISH

Preheat the grill to high. Brush the tuna steaks with the olive oil; season with salt and pepper. Lightly oil the grill if it is not non-stick, then grill the steaks for 2–3 minutes per side or until still slightly rare in the middle. (If you like your tuna entirely cooked through, cook 1–2 minutes more per side.) Spoon the chickpea salad onto the serving plates. Top each with a piece of tuna and garnish with a lemon wedge and a parsley sprig.

If desired, drizzle the fish tableside with a little extra virgin olive oil.

**ERIC'S OPTIONS**
Use other canned legumes, such as white kidney beans, instead of the chickpeas. Use other firm-fleshed fish, such as salmon or halibut.

# Maple-Mustard
# Cedar-Planked Salmon Steaks

preparation time · 10 minutes
cooking time · 20 minutes
makes · 4 servings

Sweet maple syrup balanced with tart lemon and spicy Dijon mustard adds an intriguing note to the distinctive taste of cedar planked salmon.

**NOTE**
Untreated cedar planks are sold at many supermarkets and seafood stores.

**ERIC'S OPTIONS**
Planked salmon can also be baked in the oven. Preheat the oven to 425°F (220°C). Place the plank directly on the baking rack and cook for 20 minutes, or until the salmon is just cooked through. Out of maple syrup? Use honey instead. For added texture use whole-grain Dijon mustard instead of regular.

| | | |
|---|---|---|
| 2 Tbsp. | maple syrup | 25 mL |
| 2 Tbsp. | Dijon mustard | 25 mL |
| 1/2 | lemon, juice of | 1/2 |
| 2 tsp. | chopped fresh dill | 10 mL |
| to taste | salt and freshly cracked black pepper | to taste |
| 4 | 6-oz. (175-g) salmon steaks | 4 |
| to garnish | lemon wedges and dill sprigs | to garnish |

Submerge a 12- to 14-inch (30- to 35-cm) untreated cedar plank in cold water for 2 or more hours.

Combine the maple syrup, mustard, lemon juice, dill, salt and pepper in a shallow dish. Add the salmon and turn to coat. Cover the salmon and marinate in the fridge for 30 minutes.

Preheat the grill to its highest setting. Remove the plank from the water and dry the side the fish will lie on. Set the fish on the plank.

If you have a two-burner barbecue, turn one side off when it's hot and lower the other side to medium. Place the plank on the unlit side of the barbecue. If you have a one-burner barbecue, turn it to its lowest setting before setting the plank on the grill. Close the lid and cook for about 20 minutes, or until the fish is cooked through. Keep a spray bottle of water handy just in case the board ignites. To serve, set the plank on a serving tray and garnish with lemon and dill.

# Teriyaki Salmon with Sesame Seeds and Green Onions

preparation time · 5 minutes
cooking time · 6–8 minutes
makes · 2 servings

Here's a dish with only four ingredients but a surprisingly complex flavour. Serve with steamed rice and Sesame Ginger Coleslaw (page 165).

**ERIC'S OPTIONS**
This salmon is delicious cold and makes great picnic fare. After it is grilled, place it in a container, spoon the reduced teriyaki sauce over top and sprinkle with the onions and sesame seeds. Cool to room temperature and keep refrigerated until you're ready to serve.

| | | |
|---|---|---|
| 2 | 5-oz. (150-g) salmon fillets | 2 |
| 3/4 cup | teriyaki sauce | 175 mL |
| 1 | green onion, finely chopped | 1 |
| 1 Tbsp. | sesame seeds, lightly toasted (see Note, page 128) | 15 mL |

Place the salmon in a small dish. Add 1/4 cup (50 mL) of the teriyaki sauce and turn to coat. Cover and marinate 1–2 hours, turning occasionally.

Preheat a non-stick grill to medium-high. Place the remaining 1/2 cup (125 mL) of teriyaki sauce in a small pot. Cook and reduce over medium-high heat until it's very lightly thickened. Remove from the heat and set aside. Remove the fish from the marinade; discard the marinade. Lightly oil the grill. Cook the salmon for 3–4 minutes per side, depending on the thickness, or until just cooked through. To serve, spoon some reduced teriyaki sauce over each portion. Sprinkle with green onion and sesame seeds.

# Barbecued Salmon
# with Garlic, Lemon and Herbs

preparation time · 20 minutes
cooking time · 26–30 minutes
makes · 4–6 servings

The inviting aroma from the generous amount of garlic used in this dish may cause your neighbours to peer over the backyard fence and ask, "What time is dinner?"

**ERIC'S OPTIONS:**
The salmon can also be baked in a 400°F (200°C) oven for 30 minutes, or until cooked through.

| | | |
|---|---|---|
| 1 | 3- to 4-lb. (1.5- to 2.0-kg) whole salmon | 1 |
| 1/2 cup | dry white wine | 125 mL |
| 3 Tbsp. | extra virgin olive oil | 45 mL |
| to taste | salt and freshly cracked black pepper | to taste |
| 4–6 | garlic cloves, thinly sliced | 4–6 |
| | a few sprigs dill, parsley and tarragon | |
| 1 | small lemon, sliced | 1 |

Preheat the barbecue to medium. With a sharp knife, cut off and discard the head, fins and tail of the salmon. Rinse the salmon under cold water and pat dry. Arrange 3 sheets of foil so they are slightly overlapping and are large enough to entirely encase the salmon. Place the salmon on the foil. Combine the wine and oil in a bowl. Brush some of the mixture inside the cavity of the salmon and season with salt and pepper. Stuff the cavity with the garlic, herb sprigs and lemon. Brush the outside of the salmon with the remaining wine/oil mixture and season with salt and pepper. Fold the foil over the salmon, ensuring there is a tight seal. Grill for 13–15 minutes per side, or until cooked through.

# Foil-Barbecued Clams

preparation time · 10 minutes
cooking time · 5 minutes
makes · 2 servings

The foil locks in the steam and cooking juices, making this a quick and tasty way to cook clams.

**ERIC'S OPTIONS**
Use an equal amount of mussels instead of clams. If you have a ripe medium tomato, chop it finely and add it to the wine mixture. For a more intense herb taste, replace mild-tasting parsley with basil or oregano. For a more filling meal, serve the clams on a bed of fettuccini. Served this way, the recipe will likely yield 3–4 portions, rather than 2.

| | | |
|---|---|---|
| 2 lbs. | fresh clams | 1 kg |
| 1/4 cup | dry white wine | 50 mL |
| 2 Tbsp. | melted butter | 25 mL |
| 2 | garlic cloves, crushed | 2 |
| 1 Tbsp. | chopped fresh parsley | 15 mL |
| to taste | freshly cracked black pepper | to taste |
| 1/2 | lemon, juice of | 1/2 |

Preheat the barbecue to medium-high. Cut 2 sheets of foil, each 24 x 12 inches (60 x 30 cm), and place one on top of the other. Place the clams in the centre of the foil. Pull up the edges of the foil so that when you add the liquid it won't run out. Combine the wine, butter, garlic, parsley, pepper and lemon juice in a bowl. Spoon the mixture over the clams. Seal the clams inside the foil. Grill for 5 minutes, or until the clams just open. Peek inside the foil to see how they are doing, but be careful of the hot steam. Empty into serving bowls and enjoy.

# Grilled Halibut Fillets with Wax Bean and Roma Tomato Salad

preparation time · 25 minutes
cooking time · 6–8 minutes
makes · 4 servings

The flavour of the simply seasoned halibut is accented by the colourful Mediterranean-style salad, flavoured with garlic, fresh herbs and extra virgin olive oil.

| THE SALAD | | | |
|---|---|---|---|
| | 4 | ripe Roma, or plum, tomatoes, cut into wedges | 4 |
| | 1/2 lb. | wax beans, trimmed and blanched | 250 g |
| | 1/2 | small red onion, thinly sliced | 1/2 |
| | 16–20 | black olives, whole | 16–20 |
| | 1 | garlic clove, crushed | 1 |
| | 3 Tbsp. | extra virgin olive oil | 45 mL |
| | 3 Tbsp. | balsamic vinegar | 45 mL |
| | 2 Tbsp. | chopped fresh oregano or basil | 25 mL |
| | to taste | salt and freshly cracked black pepper | to taste |

| THE FISH | | | |
|---|---|---|---|
| | 4 | 5-oz. (150-g) halibut fillets | 4 |
| | 2 Tbsp. | olive oil | 45 mL |
| | to taste | salt and freshly cracked black pepper | to taste |
| | to garnish | lemon wedges and oregano or basil sprigs | to garnish |

### THE SALAD

Combine all the ingredients in a bowl and toss gently to combine. Cover and store in the fridge until the halibut is ready.

### THE FISH

Preheat the grill to medium-high. Brush the halibut with olive oil and season with salt and pepper. Lightly oil the grill if it's not non-stick. Grill the fillets for 3–4 minutes per side, or until just cooked through.

To serve, mound the salad in the centre of individual plates. Top with the halibut. Garnish with lemon wedges and oregano or basil sprigs.

### NOTE

To blanch the wax beans, cook them in boiling water for 2 minutes. Drain well, plunge into ice-cold water, and then drain well again.

### ERIC'S OPTIONS

Use green beans instead of wax beans, or use a combination of the two. A mix of small, different-coloured tomatoes makes the salad even more colourful.

# Foil-Barbecued Halibut with Corn, Tomatoes and Dill

preparation time · 15 minutes
cooking time · 12–15 minutes
makes · 2 servings

This dish is at its best when local corn and tomatoes are in season and bursting with fresh flavour. Tiny new potatoes, boiled or steamed, go nicely with this dish.

ERIC'S OPTIONS
Use other fish, such as cod, salmon or halibut. If fresh corn is unavailable, use 1/2 cup (125 mL) of frozen corn kernels.

| | | |
|---|---|---|
| 2 Tbsp. | olive oil | 25 mL |
| 2 | 5-oz. (150-g) halibut fillets, trimmed | 2 |
| to taste | salt and freshly cracked black pepper | to taste |
| 1 | cob corn, kernels removed | 1 |
| 2 | ripe medium tomatoes, chopped | 2 |
| 2 | garlic cloves, thinly sliced | 2 |
| 1/4 cup | dry white wine | 50 mL |
| 1 Tbsp. | chopped fresh dill | 15 mL |

Preheat the barbecue to medium. Cut and overlap 2 pieces of foil, each 18 x 12 inches (45 x 30 cm). Brush the top of the foil with 1 Tbsp. (15 mL) of the oil. Place the fillets in the centre, about 2 inches (5 cm) apart. Drizzle with the remaining olive oil and season with salt and pepper.

Combine the corn, tomatoes, garlic, wine and dill in a bowl. Spoon the mixture over the fish. Fold the foil over the fish and seal the top. Grill for 12–15 minutes, or until the fish is just cooked through. Serve directly from the foil, or transfer to individual serving plates.

# Grilled Halibut Steaks
# with Pink Peppercorn Chive Butter

preparation time · 10 minutes
cooking time · 6–8 minutes
makes · 4 servings

Pink peppercorns are the dried berries of the Baies rose plant. This rose-hued spice is not a true peppercorn and doesn't have the hot bite associated with that spice. They make a mildly spicy, slightly sweet and aromatic addition to this halibut dish.

**ERIC'S OPTIONS**
Make mixed peppercorn butter by replacing half the pink peppercorns with lightly crushed green peppercorns. Replace the chives with 1 Tbsp. (15 mL) chopped fresh tarragon for a pungent licorice-scented butter.

**NOTE**
Pink peppercorns are sold dried or packed in brine or water and can be found in most supermarkets and fine food stores.

| | | |
|---|---|---|
| 1/4 lb. | butter, at room temperature | 125 g |
| 1 Tbsp. | pink peppercorns, crushed | 15 mL |
| 2 Tbsp. | chopped fresh chives | 25 mL |
| 1 | small garlic clove, crushed | 1 |
| to taste | salt and freshly cracked black pepper | to taste |
| 4 | 5-oz. (150-g) halibut fillets | 4 |
| 2 Tbsp. | olive oil | 25 mL |

Beat the butter until light. Beat in the peppercorns, chives, garlic, salt and pepper. Roll the flavoured butter in parchment paper or foil to make a log about 1 inch thick (2.5 cm) in diameter. Refrigerate until set.

Preheat the grill to medium-high. Brush the halibut with oil and season with salt and pepper. Grill the fish for 3–4 minutes per side, or until just cooked through. To serve, top each fillet with 2 thick slices of the butter and serve.

# Grilled Shark Steaks
# with Wasabi Soy Dipping Sauce

preparation time · 5 minutes
cooking time · 6–8 minutes
makes · 4 servings

For an Asian-style dinner, serve the fish with rice or egg noodles, cooked and tossed with a mix of stir-fried vegetables, such as bell peppers, bok choy, snow peas and bean sprouts, and soy or teriyaki sauce.

**ERIC'S OPTIONS**
Use other firm-fleshed fish, such as tuna, marlin or salmon, instead of shark.

| | | |
|---|---|---|
| 1/3 cup | orange juice | 75 mL |
| 2 Tbsp. | soy sauce | 25 mL |
| 1 tsp. | wasabi powder, or to taste | 5 mL |
| 2 tsp. | freshly grated ginger | 10 mL |
| 1 | garlic clove, crushed | 1 |
| 1 | green onion, finely chopped | 1 |
| 4 | 5-oz. (150-g) shark steaks | 4 |
| 1 Tbsp. | vegetable oil | 15 mL |
| to taste | salt and freshly cracked black pepper | to taste |
| to garnish | orange slices and cilantro sprigs | to garnish |

Make the sauce by mixing the orange juice, soy sauce, wasabi, ginger, garlic and green onion together in a bowl. Refrigerate until the fish is cooked.

Preheat the grill to medium-high. Brush the shark steaks with oil and season with salt and pepper. Lightly oil the grill if it's not non-stick, then grill the steaks for 3–4 minutes per side, or until just cooked through. Garnish with orange slices and cilantro. Serve the sauce in small bowls for dipping.

# Seafood
# Kebabs

| | | |
|---|---|---|
| preparation time · | 20 minutes | |
| cooking time · | 6–8 minutes | |
| makes · | 4 servings | |

These kebabs offer a pleasing mix of grilled seafood and crisp vegetables with a dash of spice. Toss together a green salad and supper is ready.

**ERIC'S OPTIONS**
For even more colourful kebabs, use a mix of red, green and yellow bell peppers. For tropical-tasting skewers, replace some of the green pepper or red onion with chunks of fresh pineapple or slightly underripe mango.

| | | |
|---|---|---|
| 2 Tbsp. | olive oil | 25 mL |
| 1/2 | lemon, juice of | 1/2 |
| pinch | cayenne pepper and sugar | pinch |
| 1 | garlic clove, crushed | 1 |
| 1/4 cup | chopped fresh basil | 50 mL |
| 8 | large sea scallops | 8 |
| 8 | large shrimp, peeled, with tail portion left intact | 8 |
| 1 | 6-oz. (170-g) salmon fillet, cut into 8 cubes | 1 |
| 1 | medium red onion, cut into 12 chunks | 1 |
| 1 | medium green bell pepper, seeded and cut into 12 chunks | 1 |
| to taste | salt and freshly cracked black pepper | to taste |

Mix the olive oil, lemon juice, cayenne pepper, sugar, garlic and basil together in a bowl. Add the scallops, shrimp and salmon and gently toss to combine. Cover and marinate in the fridge for 30 minutes.

Preheat the grill to medium. Thread the seafood, red onion and green pepper on long metal or wooden skewers, interspersing the seafood and vegetables. (If using wooden skewers, soak in cold water for several hours before threading on the ingredients to prevent scorching.) Each skewer should have 2 scallops, 2 shrimp, 2 pieces of salmon, 3 pieces of green pepper and 3 pieces of red onion. Lightly oil the grill if it's not non-stick, then grill the kebabs for 3–4 minutes per side, or until the seafood is just cooked through.

# Shrimp Satay with Sweet Chili Dipping Sauce

preparation time · 25 minutes
cooking time · 8–10 minutes
makes · 4–6 servings

Serve this sweet and spicy satay as an appetizer or make a complete meal by serving it with steamed rice and sliced onion, cucumber and tomato.

| THE SAUCE | | | |
|---|---|---|---|
| | 2 tsp. | chopped fresh ginger | 10 mL |
| | 2 tsp. | chopped garlic | 10 mL |
| | 3/4 cup | orange marmalade | 175 mL |
| | 2 Tbsp. | red wine vinegar | 25 mL |
| | 2 tsp. | soy sauce | 10 mL |
| | to taste | brown sugar | to taste |
| | 1 tsp. | hot chili sauce, or to taste | 5 mL |
| | 2 | green onions, chopped | 2 |

| THE SHRIMP | | | |
|---|---|---|---|
| | 24 | large shrimp, peeled | 24 |
| | 1 Tbsp. | brown sugar | 15 mL |
| | 1 tsp. | salt | 5 mL |
| | 1 | lime, juice of | 1 |
| | 2 tsp. | chopped fresh ginger | 10 mL |
| | 2 tsp. | chopped garlic | 10 mL |
| | 2 Tbsp. | soy sauce | 25 mL |

### THE SAUCE

Place all the ingredients in a pot and simmer for 5 minutes. Remove from the heat and set aside until the shrimp are cooked.

### THE SHRIMP

Soak 24 6-inch (15-cm) bamboo skewers in cold water for several hours to prevent them from scorching on the grill. Place the shrimp in a bowl. Add the remaining ingredients and toss to combine. Cover and marinate in the fridge for 30 minutes.

Preheat the grill to medium-high. Set the sauce over low heat to warm through. Thread 1 shrimp on the end of each skewer. Lightly oil the grill if it's not non-stick, then grill the shrimp for 1–2 minutes per side, or until just cooked through. Spoon the sauce into small dishes and serve alongside the shrimp for dipping.

ERIC'S OPTIONS
If you like cilantro, use 2–3 Tbsp. (25–45 mL) in the sauce instead of the green onions. For added texture, sprinkle the satay with toasted sesame seeds just before serving. (See Note on page 128).

NOTE
If you are unable to find 6-inch (15-cm) wooden skewers, cut the longer ones in half.

# Barbecued
# Oysters

preparation time · 5 minutes
cooking time · about 5 minutes
makes · 4 appetizer servings or 2 main-course servings

Here's a simply delicious way to cook oysters.

**ERIC'S OPTIONS**
These oysters could also be topped with the vinaigrette used in Raw Oysters with Chive Horseradish Vinaigrette (page 16).

| 12 | medium oysters in the shell | 12 |
| to garnish | lemon wedges | to garnish |
| | hot pepper sauce and horseradish | |

Preheat the barbecue to medium. Set the oysters, cupped-side down, directly on the grill. Close the lid and cook until they just open, about 5 minutes. Transfer to a platter and cool until they are safe to handle. With an oyster knife, carefully remove the top shell. Serve lemon wedges, hot sauce and horseradish alongside for squeezing, shaking and spooning on top.

# SIDES, SAUCES &BATTERS

CHAPTER NINE

# Creamy
## Coleslaw

| preparation time | · | 15 minutes |
| cooking time | · | none |
| makes | · | 4–6 servings |

This homestyle coleslaw pairs perfectly with simply grilled or battered fish. It goes particularly well with Oven-Baked Fish and Chips (page 131).

**ERIC'S OPTIONS**
Use light mayonnaise instead of regular for a fat-reduced coleslaw. Tarragon-flavoured vinegar, available at most supermarkets and fine food stores, adds an intriguing flavour note.

| | | |
|---|---|---|
| 3 cups | finely shredded cabbage | 750 mL |
| 1 | medium carrot, grated | 1 |
| 2–3 | green onions, finely chopped | 2–3 |
| 3/4 cup | mayonnaise | 175 mL |
| 1 Tbsp. | white vinegar, or to taste | 15 mL |
| 2 tsp. | sugar, or to taste | 10 mL |
| to taste | salt and white pepper | to taste |

Place all the ingredients in a bowl and toss to combine. For crisp coleslaw, serve immediately.

# Sesame Ginger Coleslaw

| preparation time | · | 15 minutes |
| cooking time | · | none |
| makes | · | 6 servings |

Serve this addictive, Japanese-style coleslaw with grilled fish or shellfish. Try it with Grilled Shark Steaks with Wasabi Soy Dipping Sauce (page 158).

**ERIC'S OPTIONS**
Prepare this coleslaw several hours in advance by making the mayonnaise mixture and the cabbage mixture and storing them in separate containers in the fridge. Combine the two just before you are ready to serve. If you are in rush, use 5 cups (1.25 L) of the prepackaged coleslaw mix sold in supermarkets instead of cutting and grating your own cabbage, carrots and green onions.

| 1/4 cup | teriyaki sauce | 50 mL |
| 1/2 cup | mayonnaise | 125 mL |
| 2 tsp. | grated ginger | 10 mL |
| 2 Tbsp. | sesame seeds, lightly toasted (see Note on page 128) | 25 mL |
| 1 tsp. | sesame oil | 5 mL |
| 4 cups | shredded green cabbage | 1 L |
| 1 cup | grated carrot | 250 mL |
| 3 | green onions, finely chopped | 3 |

Mix the teriyaki sauce, mayonnaise, ginger, sesame seeds and sesame oil together in a salad bowl. Add the cabbage, carrot and green onions and toss to combine. Serve immediately.

# Technicolour Coleslaw

preparation time · 20 minutes
cooking time · none
makes · 6–8 servings

This bright and cheery coleslaw makes a nice side dish for baked, pan-fried, deep-fried or grilled seafood. Try it with Cornmeal-Crusted Oyster Burgers (page 84).

**ERIC'S OPTIONS**
To give this coleslaw a southwestern flavour, replace the yellow bell pepper with 1 cup (250 mL) of frozen, thawed corn kernels and 1 finely chopped jalapeño pepper. Whisk 1 tsp. (5 mL) of chili powder and 1 tsp. (5 mL) of ground cumin into the dressing before adding the cabbage and other vegetables.

| | | |
|---|---|---|
| 1/4 cup | vegetable oil | 50 mL |
| 1/4 cup | apple cider vinegar | 50 mL |
| 2 Tbsp. | sugar, or to taste | 25 mL |
| 1/2 tsp. | dry mustard | 2 mL |
| to taste | salt and white pepper | to taste |
| 2 cups | finely shredded red cabbage | 500 mL |
| 2 cups | finely shredded green cabbage | 500 mL |
| 1 cup | grated carrot | 250 mL |
| 1 | medium celery rib, halved lengthwise and thinly sliced | 1 |
| 2 | green onions, finely chopped | 2 |
| 1 | medium yellow bell pepper, finely chopped | 1 |

Whisk the oil, vinegar, sugar, mustard, salt and pepper together in a salad bowl. Add the remaining ingredients and toss to combine. Allow the flavours to meld together for 20 minutes. Toss again before serving.

# Spring-Style Potato Salad

preparation time · 15 minutes
cooking time · 15–20 minutes
makes · 6 servings

This salad features ingredients traditionally associated with spring. Thanks to the global food trade, all the ingredients are available most of the year. Serve it with simply prepared seafood dishes, such as Barbecued Salmon with Lemon, Garlic and Herbs (page 152).

**ERIC'S OPTIONS**
If you like creamy potato salad, reduce the olive oil by half and mix in mayonnaise to taste when combining the dressing ingredients.

| | | |
|---|---|---|
| 2 lb. | new red or white potatoes, cut into 1-inch (2.5-cm) cubes | 1 kg |
| 1/2 lb. | asparagus, trimmed and sliced at an angle into 1/2-inch (1-cm) pieces | 250 g |
| 1/4 cup | extra virgin olive oil | 50 mL |
| 1 | lemon, juice of, or to taste | 1 |
| 1 Tbsp. | Dijon mustard | 15 mL |
| pinch | sugar | pinch |
| 2 tsp. | chopped fresh dill | 10 mL |
| to taste | salt and freshly cracked black pepper | to taste |
| 6 | medium radishes, halved lengthwise and thinly sliced | 6 |

Boil the potatoes and asparagus in separate pots until just tender. Drain well, then cool to room temperature. Whisk the oil, lemon juice, mustard, sugar and dill together in a salad bowl. Season the dressing with salt and pepper. Add the potatoes, asparagus and radishes and toss to combine.

# Saffron Rice

preparation time · 5 minutes
cooking time · about 25 minutes
makes · 4 servings

This classic rice goes great with any seafood dish, particularly those that require a starch to mop up juices—Sole with Mushroom Dill Sauce (page 138) and Seafood Sampler (page 141), for example.

**ERIC'S OPTIONS**
For even more aromatic saffron rice, replace the long-grain rice with fragrant basmati or jasmine rice.

| | | |
|---|---|---|
| 1 tsp. | saffron threads | 5 mL |
| 2 Tbsp. | olive oil | 25 mL |
| 2 | shallots, finely chopped | 2 |
| 1½ cups | long-grain white rice | 375 mL |
| 2½ cups | water, or fish or chicken stock | 625 mL |
| to taste | salt and white pepper | to taste |

Lightly crumble the saffron threads and place in a small bowl. Steep the saffron in ¼ cup (50 mL) of boiling water for 10 minutes. Heat the oil in a small pot over medium-high heat. Add the shallots and cook for 1 minute. Add the rice and cook, stirring, for 1 minute more. Add the saffron and the steeping liquid, water or stock, salt and pepper. Bring to a rapid boil, then cover, reduce the heat to its lowest setting and cook for 20 minutes, or until the rice is tender.

# Cocktail
# Sauce

preparation time · 5 minutes
cooking time · none
makes · 3/4 cup (175 mL)

Serve this tangy sauce with a range of seafood, such as raw oysters, hot or cold shrimp and deep-fried fish.

**ERIC'S OPTIONS**
Add colour and flavour to the sauce by mixing in 1 Tbsp. (15 mL) of finely chopped fresh herbs, such as dill, tarragon or chives.

| | | |
|---|---|---|
| 1/2 cup | ketchup or sweet chili sauce | 125 mL |
| 1 Tbsp. | horseradish, or to taste | 15 mL |
| 1/2 tsp. | hot pepper sauce, or to taste | 2 mL |
| 1 tsp. | Worcestershire sauce, or to taste | 5 mL |
| 1 Tbsp. | lemon juice, or to taste | 15 mL |
| to taste | salt and freshly cracked black pepper | to taste |

Combine all the ingredients in a bowl and mix well. Chill well before serving. This cocktail sauce will last a week or two in the fridge if kept in a tightly sealed container.

# Cool and Creamy Tarragon Sauce

| | |
|---|---|
| preparation time · | 5 minutes |
| cooking time · | none |
| makes · | 3/4 cup (175 mL) |

This is a great dip for cooked and chilled shrimp, crab, lobster or salmon.

**ERIC'S OPTIONS**
Try other herbs in the sauce, or a combination, such as dill, chives, parsley and cilantro. For a different look and texture, use whole-grain Dijon mustard instead of regular.

| | | |
|---|---|---|
| 1/3 cup | sour cream | 75 mL |
| 1/3 cup | mayonnaise | 75 mL |
| 1 tsp. | horseradish | 5 mL |
| 2 Tbsp. | chopped fresh tarragon | 25 mL |
| 2 tsp. | Dijon mustard | 10 mL |
| to taste | lemon juice, salt and white pepper | to taste |

Combine all the ingredients in a bowl and mix well. Chill well before serving. This sauce will last a week in the fridge if kept in a tightly sealed container.

# Tartar
# Sauce

preparation time · 5 minutes
cooking time · none
makes · 3/4 cup (175 mL)

There are a range of commercial tartar sauces sold in stores these days, but they never come close to matching the fresh and lively taste of homemade. Serve this sauce alongside simply prepared seafood or on seafood burgers.

**ERIC'S OPTIONS**
For a less sharp sauce, use sweet mixed pickles instead of dill pickles. If you don't have tarragon or don't care for its licorice-like taste, use dill or parsley instead.

| | | |
|---|---|---|
| 1/2 cup | mayonnaise | 125 mL |
| 2 Tbsp. | finely chopped dill pickle | 25 mL |
| 1 | green onion, finely chopped | 1 |
| 1 Tbsp. | drained capers, coarsely chopped | 15 mL |
| 1 Tbsp. | chopped fresh parsley | 15 mL |
| 1 tsp. | lemon juice | 5 mL |
| 1 tsp. | Dijon mustard | 5 mL |
| 1 tsp. | chopped fresh tarragon, or pinch dried | 5 mL |
| to taste | salt, white pepper and hot pepper sauce | to taste |

Combine all the ingredients in a bowl and mix well. Chill before serving. This sauce will last a week in the fridge if kept in a tightly sealed container.

# Japanese-Style Ginger Sauce

| | | |
|---|---|---|
| preparation time | · | 5 minutes |
| cooking time | · | none |
| makes | · | 2/3 cup (150 mL) |

Try this dipping sauce with grilled, steamed or deep-fried seafood. It goes particularly well with simply grilled or steamed large shrimp, served hot or cold or cooked in Tempura Batter (page 180).

**ERIC'S OPTIONS**
For added colour and flavour, mix 1–2 Tbsp. (15–25 mL) of finely chopped chives or cilantro into the sauce. For added texture and flavour, mix in 1–2 Tbsp. (15–25 mL) of lightly toasted sesame seeds. (See Note on page 128).

| 1/2 cup | mayonnaise | 125 mL |
|---|---|---|
| 1 tsp. | grated fresh ginger | 5 mL |
| 2 Tbsp. | teriyaki sauce, or to taste | 25 mL |
| 1 tsp. | wasabi powder, or to taste | 5 mL |

Place all the ingredients in a bowl and whisk to combine. Cover and allow the flavours to meld in the fridge for 30 minutes. This sauce will last for a week in the fridge if kept in a tightly sealed container.

# Mango
# Salsa

preparation time · 10 minutes
cooking time · none
makes · about 1 1/2 cups (375 mL)

Serve this tropical-tasting salsa with grilled seafood, such as Seafood Kebabs (page 159).

**ERIC'S OPTIONS**
Substitute a papaya for the mango for a different tropical taste. To make tomato salsa, replace the mango with 2–3 medium ripe tomatoes, seeded and chopped.

| | | |
|---|---|---|
| 1 | ripe medium mango, peeled and cut into 1/4-inch (5-mm) cubes | 1 |
| 1/4 cup | finely diced red onion | 50 mL |
| 1/4 cup | finely diced green bell pepper | 50 mL |
| 2–3 Tbsp. | chopped cilantro | 25–45 mL |
| 1 | large lime, juice of or to taste | 1 |
| 2 tsp. | warm honey, or to taste | 10 mL |
| pinch | crushed chili flakes | pinch |
| to taste | salt and white pepper | to taste |

Combine all the ingredients in a bowl and mix well. Cover and allow the flavours to meld for 30 minutes at room temperature. Gently mix again before serving.

# White Wine Chive Sauce

preparation time · 5 minutes
cooking time · 5–6 minutes
makes · about 1 cup (250 mL)

This basic sauce adds richness to mild-tasting fish fillets, such as sole, cod or flounder.

**ERIC'S OPTIONS**
Replace the chives with other herbs, such as dill or parsley. Make saffron sauce by adding 1/4 tsp. (1 mL) of saffron threads to the wine before reducing it. Make Champagne sauce by replacing the white wine with an equal amount of Champagne or sparkling wine. Make grainy mustard white wine sauce, which pairs nicely with stronger-tasting fish such as salmon, by adding 1–2 Tbsp. (15–25 mL) of whole-grain Dijon mustard to the sauce after the whipping cream has been added and the sauce has thickened.

| | | |
|---|---|---|
| 1/2 cup | white wine | 125 mL |
| 1 cup | whipping cream | 250 mL |
| 1 Tbsp. | chopped fresh chives | 15 mL |
| to taste | salt and white pepper | to taste |

Place the wine in a saucepan and bring to a boil. Cook until it's reduced by half. Add the whipping cream and continue cooking until the sauce thickens slightly. Stir in the chives and season with salt and pepper. Serve warm.

# Black and Green
# Olive Relish

preparation time · 15 minutes
cooking time · none
makes · about 1 cup (250 mL)

Serve a generous spoonful of this vibrant, Mediterranean-style relish alongside grilled fish, such as tuna, marlin or salmon. Try it with Grilled Tuna on Chickpea Salad (page 148) or use the relish to top fish fillets before baking.

**ERIC'S OPTIONS**
Use the relish to make seafood canapés. Lightly toast rounds of baguette and spread them generously with the relish. Top with salad shrimp, crabmeat or grilled, cooled and sliced scallops; garnish with a small basil or oregano sprig. Make the relish spicy by adding crushed chili flakes to taste.

| | | |
|---|---|---|
| 1/2 cup | pitted black olives, finely chopped | 125 mL |
| 1/2 cup | pitted green olives, finely chopped | 125 mL |
| 4 | anchovy fillets, finely chopped | 4 |
| 1/4 cup | extra virgin olive oil, or to taste | 50 mL |
| 2 Tbsp. | capers, coarsely chopped | 25 mL |
| 2 | garlic cloves, finely chopped | 2 |
| 2 Tbsp. | chopped fresh basil or oregano | 25 mL |
| 1/2 tsp. | grated lemon zest | 2 mL |
| 1 Tbsp. | lemon juice | 15 mL |
| to taste | freshly cracked black pepper | to taste |

Combine all the ingredients in a bowl and mix well. Store in a tightly sealed container in the fridge until needed; it will keep for a week or two. Warm to room temperature before serving.

# Green
## Goddess Dressing

preparation time · 15 minutes
cooking time · none
makes · about 1 1/4 cups (300 mL)

Serve this classic dressing on salads or as a dip with raw vegetables or pan-fried and deep-fried fish and shellfish. It also tastes great with seafood cakes.

**ERIC'S OPTIONS**
If you're not handy with a knife, coarsely chop the herbs, anchovies, green onions and garlic. Place in a food processor and pulse until finely chopped.

| | | | |
|---|---|---|---|
| 1/2 cup | mayonnaise | 125 mL |
| 1/4 cup | sour cream | 50 mL |
| 1/4 cup | finely chopped fresh parsley | 50 mL |
| 1 Tbsp. | finely chopped fresh tarragon, or 1 tsp. (5 mL) dried | 15 mL |
| 1 Tbsp. | finely chopped anchovy fillets | 15 mL |
| 2 | green onions, finely chopped | 2 |
| 1 | garlic clove, finely chopped | 1 |
| to taste | salt, white pepper and lemon juice | to taste |

Place all the ingredients in a bowl with 2–3 Tbsp. (25–45 mL) of cold water. Mix well to combine. Allow the flavours to meld for at least 30 minutes in the fridge before serving. Store the dressing in a tightly sealed container in the fridge for up to one week.

### THE MATH ON ANCHOVY FILLETS AND PASTE

Anchovy paste is usually not as strong in flavour as canned anchovies, but it is frequently saltier and often contains other ingredients. Consider the following when you're deciding how much of the canned fillets to buy or whether to substitute with anchovy paste.

• A 2-oz. (50-g) can of anchovies contains 7 to 10 fillets and yields 3 Tbsp. (45 mL) of chopped or mashed anchovy.

• 1 anchovy fillet equals $1/2$ tsp. (2 mL) anchovy paste.

• 1 tsp. (5 mL) of chopped or mashed anchovy equals 1 tsp. (5 mL) of anchovy paste, or to taste, keeping in mind that the paste is often milder in flavour than whole fillets.

# Spicy Anchovy Butter

| | | |
|---|---|---|
| preparation time | · | 10 minutes |
| cooking time | · | none |
| makes | · | 1/2 cup (125 mL) |

Use slices of this hot and salty butter as a topping for grilled fish fillets or steaks.

**ERIC OPTIONS**
Make jalapeño anchovy butter by replacing the crushed chili flakes with 1–2 Tbsp. (15–25 mL) of finely chopped canned or fresh jalapeño peppers. Or use a more flavourful herb, such as basil, tarragon or oregano instead of parsley.

| | | |
|---|---|---|
| 1/2 cup | butter, at room temperature | 125 mL |
| 1 Tbsp. | anchovy paste | 15 mL |
| 1/2 tsp. | crushed chili flakes | 2 mL |
| 1 Tbsp. | chopped fresh parsley | 15 mL |

Beat all the ingredients together until light and well combined. Place on a sheet of plastic wrap or foil and form into a log 2 inches (5 cm) wide. Refrigerate until firm. The butter will keep about a week in the fridge and a month in the freezer. Warm to just below room temperature before using. Slice into 1/4-inch-thick (5-mm) disks and set on top of grilled fish fillets or steaks as soon as they come off the grill.

# Canadian
# Beer Batter

preparation time · 5 minutes
cooking time · none
makes · enough to coat 6–8 fish fillets

Foamy beer adds lightness and tanginess to batter. Use this to coat your favourite fish fillet before deep-frying.

**ERIC'S OPTIONS**
For darker, richer-tasting batter use dark ale instead of lager. For a peppery taste, add 2 tsp. (10 mL) of coarsely cracked black pepper to the batter.

| | | |
|---|---|---|
| 1 cup | Canadian lager | 250 mL |
| 1 | large egg, beaten | 1 |
| 2 Tbsp. | vegetable oil, plus more for frying | 25 mL |
| 1 Tbsp. | freshly squeezed lemon juice | 15 mL |
| 1 tsp. | grated lemon zest | 5 mL |
| 3/4–1 cup | all-purpose flour | 175–250 mL |
| 1/2 tsp. | salt | 2 mL |
| 1/8 tsp. | white pepper | .5 mL |
| 1 tsp. | baking powder | 5 mL |

Whisk the beer, egg, oil, lemon juice and zest together in a bowl. Whisk together the flour, salt, white pepper and baking powder in another bowl. Mix the flour mixture into the egg mixture until a slightly lumpy batter forms. (To use, heat the oil in your deep-fat fryer to 350–375°F [180–190°C]. Coat fish fillets with flour, shaking off any excess. Dip the fillets in the batter, coating them evenly. Deep-fry the fish for 4–5 minutes, or until golden brown and cooked through.)

# Tempura
# Batter

preparation time · 5 minutes
cooking time · none
makes · enough to coat 6–8 fish fillets,
12 medium oysters or 24 large shrimp

Use this Japanese-style batter to give deep-fried fish fillets and shellfish such as peeled shrimp and shucked oysters, a light, wispy, crunchy coating.

**ERIC'S OPTIONS**
Make coconut tempura batter by mixing in 1/4 cup (50 mL) of medium, unsweetened coconut flakes. Coconut gives the batter an interesting, chewy texture and slightly sweet taste.

| | | |
|---|---|---|
| 1 1/4 cups | ice-cold water | 300 mL |
| 1 | egg yolk | 1 |
| 1 cup | all-purpose flour | 250 mL |

Place the water and egg yolk in a bowl and whisk to combine. Whisk in the flour until a slightly lumpy batter forms. (To use, heat the oil in your deep-fat fryer to 350–375°F [180–190°C]. Dip the seafood into the batter, allowing the excess to drain away. Cook the seafood until crisp, very light golden in colour and cooked through.)

# Index

# About
## the Author

Eric Akis has been the food writer for the Victoria *Times Colonist* for the past eight years. He has written and created recipes for over 350 food columns, many of which have been published in other newspapers across Canada.

When he's not writing, Eric works as a food consultant, offering services such as food styling, recipe development and food-related concept development. His principal client the last six years has been Thrifty Foods, Vancouver Island's largest super-market chain, recently named one of Canada's 50 Best Managed Companies.

Prior to becoming a food writer and consultant he worked in professional kitchens for 15 years, in a diverse range of establishments. He is a certified chef and pastry chef, both with honours, and has furthered his business acumen by obtaining a certificate in business administration from the University of Victoria.

Eric was born in Chicoutimi, Quebec. Because his late father was in the military, he moved often and feels at home in many regions of the country. Victoria, British Columbia, is now officially home, where he lives with his wife, Cheryl, and son, Tyler.

His favourite way to relax, even though he cooks almost every day to earn his keep, is to prepare his family a delicious meal every night—except for Sunday, when his wife takes over the kitchen and he goes to the pub for a pre-dinner pint or two.

This is Eric Akis's second book. His first, *Everyone Can Cook*, became a Canadian best-seller soon after its release.